S0-AEH-780

kopernik

**ABDÜLKADİR ÖZKAN:** Journalist and writer. He was born in 1980 in Istanbul. He graduated from Istanbul Bilgi University, Faculty of Communication. He began his journalism career at *Yörünge* journal as a reporter in 1993. He worked as a foreign news editor at İhlas News Agency. After working as a news coordinator for *Turkish News Weekly* in Sydney, Australia for two years, he worked as a news editor in Thailand, Hong Kong, China and Indonesia. He lived in Lebanon, Jordan and Dubai for three years, right after the assassination of Lebanon's Prime Minister Refik Hariri. He continued to write weekly columns in the *TNW*. He served as editor-in-chief of the *Global Research* journal. His expertise lies in media and intercultural relations and Marshall McLuhan's theories on media. He served as the press adviser to Professor Mehmet Görmez, director of the Presidency of Religious Affairs, in 2010, and as the press counselor to Professor Nabi Avcı, minister of education in 2014. He was appointed as chief adviser to the prime minister in 2015. Currently, he is a board member of the Turkish National Commission for UNESCO, general secretary of the Islamic Culture and Arts Platform, board member of the European Diplomats Association, director of the Cultural and Arts Studies Center, and general secretary of the Democracy for Everyone Enterprise. He has good command of English. He is married with three children.

First published by Kopernik Publishing House
®Abdülkadir Özkan 2017

All rights reserved to Abdülkadir Özkan and Dolmabahçe AŞ. Except for short
excerpts for promoting purposes, it can not be distributed electronically or me-
chanically without the permission of the author or the publisher. All the rights of
this book are reserved to the author.

Editor in Chief: Abdülkadir Özkan
Advisor: Prof. Halil Berktay
Series Editor: Mehmet Erdoğan
Visual Director: Osman Özkan
Final Editing: Gönül Taban
Cover Design: Ali Kaya
Application:Tavoos

Kopernik Publishing House
Dolmabahçe AŞ
Altunizade Mah. Ord. Prof. Fahrettin Kerim Gökay Cad.34 Üsküdar
ISTANBUL
www.kopernikkitap.com

Certification no: 35175
ISBN: 978-975-2439-08-5
First Edition: May 2017
Third Edition: August 2017

Publishing and Volume
Bilnet Matbaacılık ve Yayıncılık A.Ş.
Umraniye/Istanbul

Kopernik Publishing House is a trade mark of Dolmabahçe AŞ
ISTANBUL • LONDON • NEW YORK

# THE MODERN ASSASSIN

## GULENIST CULT AND
## FETULLAH GULEN'S SECRET AGENDA

ABDULKADIR OZKAN

kopernik

*To Erol Olçok, his son and all our glorified martyrs who lost their lives on the night of July 15...*

# CONTENTS

# INTRODUCTION

Turkey's history after 1960 can be considered the history of coups. The dominant political actor of the time for almost a period of sixty years was the junta that was established in 1957, and exerted its power after the 1960s.

In that time period, there were eleven coups/coup attempts, most of which took place during my childhood. I studied several of them due to my profession. Three of the attempts happened in 1962, 1963, and on March 9, 1971; there was one military intervention on March 12, 1971, one in 1980 and others in 1987, on February 28, 1997, on April 27, 2007, on February 7, 2012, on December 17 and December 25, 2013, and finally on July 15, 2016. These are the ones that had surfaced. Yet, nobody knows the actual number of unsuccessful attempts.

When I asked to the late Turgut Özal, "Don't you feel anxious about this arrogance?" pointing the man in uniform who had insulted him, his answer was no different to the one he gave on the day of his assassination attempt: "One cannot live in a permanent state of anxiety. Only God can take the life that He gave!"

All the coups and coup attempts I had enlisted above are, without a doubt, very important and left deep scars on the

Turkish state. However, in the midst of all this, it is impossible not to recognize that coups and coup attempts gained new momentum in the time of one leader and his government.

It is unknown whether or not it was thought that Recep Tayyip Erdoğan would be such a determining figure in the Turkish political world when he began his political career. What is known is that he was accepted by the public from the start. Being able to establish direct communication with the people and his sincere rhetoric carried Erdoğan to a special place not just in Turkish politics but also in global political domain. Continuously increasing his public support in elections, and not having any other comparable political figure in Turkish politics is indeed a quite striking phenomenon. Erdoğan's most important characteristics are his legitimacy-minded personality and powerful intuitions. If Turkey got out of the April 27 memorandum stronger, or was able overcome the December 17/25 coup attempts, it is because of Recep Tayyip Erdoğan's intuitions, his ability of political analysis and his self-esteem.

Finally, the July 15, 2016 coup attempt... Recep Tayyip Erdoğan is the symbol of an unprecedented resistance in the last 2,000 years of Turkish history. His resistance against the coup plotters, despite the fact that he had every chance to run away, can only be described as epic. On that night, he had no military power ready under his hand, a significant portion of the army was part of the rebellion; he was alienated even by his most loyal guards, and both his own life as well as his family's were at stake.

In passing, I would like to relate an anecdote. It is Recep Tayyip Erdoğan's call that convinced people to take active part on the night of July 15. After the end of the disastrous WWI, Ottoman high officials and soldiers gathered at the big hall of

Dolmabahçe Palace. They were waiting to see Sultan Vahdettin. In the meantime, one of the soldiers said, "Our army did not have enough courage at war. Many of them fled from the battle field." Mustafa Kemal was one of the people gathered at the hall. He could not help himself and said, "Turkish soldiers would not flee. If someone fled from the battle field, it must have been the commander!"

Recep Tayyip Erdoğan's example reminds us of this anecdote. The public had resisted, got injured and died. However, they knew that there was a leader who was ready to sacrifice his life if deemed necessary.

Each and every study that examines the story of the June 15 coup attempt is worthy of praise. My fellow Abdülkadir Özkan's book is an important work as it analyzes the main culprit of the coup attempt, FETÖ's structural organization. In this regard, the book should be considered as a historical document. I congratulate my friend for this comprehensive and conscientious work and hope that it will pave the way for further work on FETÖ and other similar organizations.

**Avni ÖZGÜREL**

# FOREWORD

This is neither a biography nor a memoir. It is a comprehensive news file created after meticulous work that reveals the true nature of a mysterious individual who left his imprint on the Turkish public and political life.

This is the story of a "preacher" who emerged during very tough times when efforts were made to destroy religion and religiosity; thinking, believing and speaking about religion were banned, and believers were obliged to seek to practice their religion through illegal and abusive groups. This work includes an educational lesson on a man who worked as a manager for international intelligence agencies' global Islamization project, and sold out his country and people for the sake of fulfilling his selfish goals. At the same time, it is both the exemplary and sad story of an "organization leader" who used religion, pious people, freedom and democracy in the name of his own 'values.' It is the story of the sharp turns he took in life, and the lies and paradoxes on which he built his life. It is a horrific story of the modern version of Hassan Sabbah's bloody empire which built everything on lies, and in which radical Islam evolved in to moderate Islam, eventually turning in to a terrorist organization that has dark and uncanny relations.

In this work, which is based on careful examination of numerous Turkish and international sources on Fetullah Gülen, you will read about Gülen's paradoxical rhetoric, principles of his secrets, his ambition for power and authority, and his affection for intelligence (espionage). In this work you will also find important segments from the paradoxical life of Gülen, who emptied the meaning of all traditional and modern concepts, who feels no need to hide his admiration for the West, and who explained all of his controversial political and religious statements with convenience. The last section will discuss Gülen's report card on democracy, and who are behind the rising anti-Turkey sentiments in the West after July 15, 2016.

This study does not aim to cover Fetullah Gülen's complete life story. It is an important mission to document this dangerous character, who built his entire life on paradoxes, and to protect people from other similar dangers.

I present my endless gratitude to my dear Professor Nabi Avcı who encouraged me to complete this work; to my friends Mehmet Erdoğan and Mehmet Akar who did not hesitate to extend their support and criticism; and to my dear wife, Nurbanu, my daughters and son, whom I neglected during my intensive and sleepless working days and nights. Without their encouragement and contributions, this work would not have been possible.

*December 2016 – Çankaya*
**Abdülkadir ÖZKAN**

# CHAPTER I
## TWO DIFFERENT PORTRAITS

# FROM A RELIGIOUS LEADER TO A TERRORIST LEADER

Fetullah Gülen, a mysterious name that was discussed extensively in recent years. He was subjected to significant allegations, and has a secret web of dark relations. There has been a significant amount of literature on Gülen, both positive and negative. For some he is a preacher, an imam, the "Hocaefendi", an opinion leader, a negotiator, and toward the end of his life time, a wise man. From another point of view, he is the leader of an organization, the head of terrorists, a murderer with blood on his hands, a false prophet, false guardian, secret cardinal, a universal imam who tries to conquer the world, a camouflaged Bahai leader, intelligence agent, and a multi-millionaire education tycoon. It is very noteworthy to have different and completely opposite portraits. These two very different perspectives on him did not emerge after the failed coup attempt of July 15. In recent years, very serious articles were published on Western Europe and the Unites States, depicting the Gülen Movement as a threat with international intelligence connections. Another important detail is that all these articles were written by people who have knowledge on the FBI and CIA's dirty relations. Since it is not possible for the two opposite pictures to be true at the same time, the true picture and naked truth can only be found by analyzing books written by Gülen, his private and public speeches, legal records of his statements in both Turkish and American courts, and his media declarations. What kind of a mental and spiritual state does the secret name at the center of debates have? How does he influence his followers? What does he have in his secret agenda? What kind of relations does he have with intelligence services? What is he aiming to achieve with the billions of dollars in funds he has? How does he hide his paradoxical rhetoric in the West and the United states to reach his goals? Why is he involved in trade and politics? Why is it that a preacher who was born in Erzurum, worked for a long time as state official, became a resident of Saylorsburg, Pennsylvania and runs a billion-dollar fund that has connections in 165 different countries? It is possible to answer these questions correctly solely by presenting tangible proofs that are far from conspiracy theories and extremism.

## Who is this Fetullah Gülen?

It would be useful to look at Fetullah Gülen's life before analyzing his rhetoric. There are different accounts about Gülen's birthday. According to his statement, he was born in 1941 in the village of Korucuk in Erzurum's Pasinler town.

He is the second child of an imam's eight children – six boys and two girls. He started to receive religious education in 1945 through his father. It holds an extensive place in his memory because of a murder case[1] in which his family was involved in 1945. His family moved to the village of Alvar and he had to drop out of primary school.[2] Due to some problems, he graduated from primary school as a distance student. Between 1955

---

[1]  Ergün Poyraz, *İhanet ve Darbe*, Bilgi Yayınevi, Istanbul 2016, p. 51.
[2]  Latif Erdoğan, *Fethullah Gülen, Küçük Dünyam*, Ufuk Yayınları, Istanbul 2006, p. 110

and 1959, he received intensive madrassah education and was appointed as an imam in 1959 to the *Üç Şerefeli Mosque* in Edirne. After serving for four years in Edirne, he left for Ankara and İskenderun for his military service. He returned to Erzurum after finishing his military service. Instead of resuming work as an imam, he worked for a while as the head of the Struggle Against Communism Association in 1963.

He was appointed as preacher to Kırklareli in 1965 and to İzmir in 1966. The famous 'Kestanepazarı sermons' for which he gained his fame started as a result of this appointment. During his appointments, the help of *"Nurcu"* Yaşar Tunagür, a former vice president of the Presidency of Religious Affairs, cannot be disregarded. It is great coincidence that Gülen's first contact with the CIA chief of Turkey and the Middle East took place in those days. Gülen was arrested and stayed in prison for seven months during the 1971 memorandum. He was appointed as preacher of Edirne in 1972, and then continued his sermons in Manisa and İzmir. In the meantime, he began to give conferences in various towns of Anatolia.

After the 1980 coup there was a warrant for Gülen, and he resigned from his post at the Presidency of Religious Affairs in 1981. He started to write lead articles in the *Sızıntı* and *Yeni Ümit* journals. He performed the pilgrimage in 1986 and then in 1989, he started to work as an honorary preacher for the Presidency of Religious Affairs. In the 1990s, he held meetings with famous statesmen and religious individuals such as Turgut Özal, Tansu Çiller, Mesut Yılmaz, Bülent Ecevit, Abraham Foxman, Morton Abramowitz, and Pope John Paul II. Another interesting thing happened in these years. To fulfill the will of Republican People's Party's (CHP) former Secretary General Kasım Gülek[3], who

---

[3] The daily *Yeni Şafak, dated* March 30, 2015, published a series of documents, showing that Gülen was awarded a medal of honor by the Turkish Masonic Lodge, for

was residing in the US, Gülen led the funeral prayer at Ankara Kocatepe Mosque. Gülen's activities became visible in media in the 1990s. Following the post-modern coup of February 28, he began to reside in Pennsylvania, US, where he went for the first time for his health condition. In 2000, he was accused by the State Security Court (DGM). Nuh Mete Yüksel, chief prosecutor of the Republic, prepared a bill of indictment, accusing him of *"Attempting to collapse the Republic of Turkey."* In a survey conducted by *Foreign Policy in 2008,* Gülen's name was mentioned among the *"World's top 100 Intellectuals"* alongside Bernard Lewis, Jürgen Habermas, Umberto Eco, and Noam Chomsky. In the same year Gülen, was about to be deported from the US due to an FBI investigation. However, he was granted unlimited residency as "highly gifted, with the guarantee of some Americans, such as Graham Fuller. In 2003, *Times* published an issue with Gülen as one of the "World's Most Influential 100 People." The government's decision to close down extracurricular private teaching institutions (dershane) as a part of its educational reform, led to a ruthless war between Gülen and the AK Party. Today, we see Gülen, who targets President Recep Tayyip Erdoğan directly, both as instigator and perpetrator of the July 15 coup attempt and the leader of a terrorist organization.

## Paradoxes in his Rhetoric

After this brief background, let's take a look at his rhetoric, embedded in his sermons and private gatherings on various occasions. In the early the 1990s, Gülen gave important advice to his followers. He saw the state as a device that must

his services. According to the documents, he was initated to the Masonic lodge in 1975. As seen in Kasım Gülek's letter, Gülen received the greatest medal, which is "every Mason's dream". In those days, Gülen regularly participated in the Masonic 'brotherly table' meetings held at the Tenis Eskrim ve Dağcılık Kulübü, to share 'salt and bread' with his brothers.

be captured and hence instructed his followers *"To continue their work in great secrecy until they are powerful enough to carry the world."* He told his followers that they needed to target not only Turkey but the whole world and said:

*"The day we settle accounts with the world will come..."*

"The world lives in the ages of pharaohs. The conditions are quite appropriate to destroy the pharaoh. Until the moment we find our essence, we reach maturity, until the moment we are powerful enough to carry the world on our shoulders, until the moment we seize all that represents power, until the moment we take over all constitutional institutions, every step is early, every step is like cracking an egg before it completes its twenty-day period. It is like leaving incubation, it is like leaving the chicks out in a hurricane, in hail, and this is what is being done there. What is done here is the settlement of accounts with the world at the micro level. It is the settlement of accounts with an entire world and, it is these people, who will one day settle scores with the world, learning the ways to settle scores with the world It is practice and discipline. The ones that go through the mills of life will construct their own world as the workers of the future, and will be the architects of opinions. However, those who do not go through the mills of life repeatedly, will be the victims of their own inexperience and ineptness, and naturally, they will be harmed in their own country. This is us, this is our voice and I described this world, amid all this crowd, in secrecy. I know that – like the juice boxes you will be dumping in the trash as you leave –you will throw these thoughts in the trash. Am I making myself clear? Your secrecy is your slave. The moment you share a secret, you become its slave."[4]

---

[4]  Nusret Senem, *Fethullah Gülen'in Konuşmaları ve Pensilvanya İfadesi,* Kaynak Yayınları, Istanbul 2012, pp 14-15.

While he gives the codes of a utopic project of "conquering the world" to his followers in his private sermons, he answers questions like "Do you have political aims?" "Have you ever tried to get yourself or others into governmental positions?" asked by the US State Attorney on November 6, 2001 in New Jersey as follows:

> *"I never even thought of changing the Turkish Constitution ever..."*

"With God's will and permission I have only one purpose. To win God's appreciation, to make people know and love God, and to act with God's permission and His holy name.

*Question:* Have you ever tried to get yourself or others into governmental positions?

*FG:* No. On the contrary, in my thirty-year experience in giving sermons at mosques, I was criticized greatly for being very statist by others. I am someone who declares the state and government are almost sacred.

*Question:* But this does not answer the question. Did you ever try to get yourself or others into governmental positions?

*FG:* I never had such an ambition or made such an attempt. However, I always wanted people with honor and dignity to work as state officials. I had no other attempt than this.

*Question:* Well, did you ever make any effort to change people in the government?

*FG:* Not even for myself. I cannot even think about such a thing, not even in my dreams. And I must add, when I was 25 they came to my door and proposed that I become a member of Parliament, but I chose to be close to God and work for God's sake rather than being in that position.

*Question:* Did you try to change the secular nature of the state?

*FG:* I never had such an intention. I never even think about such a thing.

*Question:* Did you ever try to change the Constitution of the Turkish state?

*FG:* Such thoughts never came to my mind. I never thought about it.

*Question:* Do/Did you ever try to incorporate religious principles in the state, I mean Islamic principles?

*FG:* Not even on the surface. On the contrary, I regard this as disrespectful.

*Question:* Did you ever try to bring down the Turkish government?

*FG:* I shudder when I hear such things.

*Question:* Did you try it or not? Yes or no?

*FG:* Absolutely, absolutely no."[5]

We see Gülen answering the questions of the American State attorney based on criminal charges of the 2nd State Security Court of Ankara 2000/124, trying intensely to give the impression to his addressees that he is a cleric who lives an ascetic life. He refutes charges of aiming to capture state mechanism through installing his followers in critical positions and claims that they have no political aims, that his only objective is to live a life devoted to attaining God's pleasure. The same Gülen, in one of his private sermons, accepts that he has followers in the Justice Department and civil service,

---

[5]   Senem, *Fethullah Gülen'in Konuşmaları ve Pensilvanya İfadesi,* pp 90-92.

saying, "the presence of [his] friends in the Justice and Civil Service departments are a guarantee for the future". Contrary to his statements claiming that he is not involved in politics he confesses that "In his twenties, he had made plans to bring down the government".

### *"You cannot reach your goals by clashing with the state..."*

"This people of the world are fools, for they do not understand us, and say "they demand power etc"... Are they crazy? Why would I be busy with such small things? What is the thing you call power? I am someone who planned to bring it down in my twenties....[6] The existence of our friends in Justice, Civil Service and other critical departments are not individual cases. They are our future in those departments. In a way, they are the guarantee of our existence."[7]

You cannot reach your goals by clashing with the state. For, the state needs to reach a point for realization of these very high goals. We can say that, in some ways, the state had reached that point. All the different opinions you have on evaluating the situation, does not mean you be a blind enemy of the state and have a conflicting attitude towards the state. We are servants of a universal message"[8]

"In this system our friends will walk to future. Therefore, they are obliged to learn the key parts of the system. We have friends in the Justice Department and Civil Service Department as well. Wherever they are, they need to work freely and prosper. If they are a district governor, they strive to become a provincial governor; if they are an

---

[6]  https://www.youtube.com/watch?v=yf0P_80Jlxk
[7]  Necip Hablemitoğlu, *Köstebek*, Pozitif Yayıncılık, Istanbul 2016, pp 20-22.
[8]  Hablemitoğlu, *Köstebek*, p. 23.

ordinary judge, they should strive to become a prestigious judge. They should be in dialogue with everyone, and never clash with political powers and people even if they are 100 percent against us...."[9]

Gülen, in his books that he later revised because of reactions, gives his followers important messages between the lines:

> "We are climbing a hill with a heavy load and we have lots of enemies who cannot tolerate to see us at the pinnacle..."[10] "... It is very risky for men of cause to act individually. It is closed and a subtle betrayal to our cause."[11] "Similar to Hitler, who places his tanks in the Russian swamp for those who come after them to step on them and cross the swamp during World War II, one generation needs to sacrifice itself for the salvation of the future generations."[12]

> "Everyone who serves Islam is a soldier. Hence, in this service military discipline is crucial. We are not soldiers in form but spiritually we are and we should be. For this reason, anyone who cannot understand the idea that he is a soldier at the service of Islam, and act in awareness of this will absolutely and surely pay a cost for it..."[13]

## Abraham Wagner discovers the "Secret Game"

Let's take a break from the paradoxes in Fetullah Gülen's rhetoric and take a look at *The Washington Times* writer Abra-

---

[9] Can Özçelik, *Kâinat İmamı Fethullah Gülen*, Destek Yayınları, Istanbul 2014, p. 154.
[10] Fethullah Gülen, *İnanan Gölgesinde 2*, Nil Yayınları, İzmir 1993, p. 234.
[11] Fethullah Gülen, *Fasıldan Fasıla 3*, Nil Yayınları, İzmir 2009, p. 69.
[12] Fethullah Gülen, *Prizma 2*, Nil Yayınları, İzmir 2010, p. 110.
[13] Fethullah Gülen, *Fasıldan Fasıla 1*, Nil Yayınları, İzmir 2006, p. 125.

ham Wagner's January 2016 article entitled, "When Moderation hides Radical Agenda," that "discovers sneaky and radical agenda". Wagner, considers the FBI's inaction towards Gülen, who continues to work to bring down the Turkish government, contrary to American interests:

> *"Gülen Movement continues to pose a threat to the USA and Turkey..."*

"Nobody would like to experience the Cosby situation in which one's all suspicious and bad acts are disclosed to the world. Gülen Movement's irresponsible leader Fetullah Gülen experienced this Cosby situation through FBI.

Primary school graduate Turkish man of religion Gülen, is a mysterious personality. In the documents revealed by Wikileaks, the Foreign Secretary depicts Gülen as 'radical Islamist' who hides his sneaky and radical agenda'. Although it is thought that Gülen is ruling a fortune of 25 billion dollars, nobody knows where the money is coming from. Despite the views of American Foreign Secretary, Gülen especially promotes tolerance and multiculturalism. However, when analyzed closely, Gülen is a real and pure radical Islamist who wants to turn Turkey and the USA to an Islamic State run by Sharia.

Gülen rules highly debated wide web of private schools along with interrelated non-profit institutions and businesses from the USA where he spends his voluntary exile. According to American and Turkish evidences presented to the courts, Gülen is planning and encouraging actively to topple down the democratically elected government of Turkey, which is one of the few stable allies of the United States in the Middle East and a NATO member that has the key importance in defeating ISIS and bring peace to Iraq...

Gülen Movement is constantly under investigation in the States due to their secret attempts to infiltrate to all spheres of the government including security forces and judiciary to change constitutional system and topple down the democratically elected government. Turkish prosecutors and police officers that are directed by Gülen movement, with false accusation and types that are acquired illegally, targeted senior military personnel and put secular journalists that are not following a strict Islamic way into jail.

From geopolitical point of view, a broadened investigation will reveal the fact that 'radical Islamist' Gülen is hiding his sneaky and radical agenda by moderate messages that American Secretary of State already knows. This investigation will also reveal Fetullah Gülen's plans to topple down the Turkish government and if Gülen would be successful in his attempt to bring down the government Turkey will be following a path contrary to American interest. Quite simply, United States does not need a Gülenist regime that rules important NATO ally in world's one of the most critical regions."[14]

Thanks to Wagner, we acquire the latest information on the point Gülen achieved in the field of education. One important point needs to be underlined here. It is understood that approximately six months before the July 15 coup attempt, Wagner realized that Gülen was determined to bring down the government and his followers are working in this extent. Is it possible that Wagner's observations would not be taken into account by White House or President Obama? Or is it possible for the CIA to overlook this detail realized by Wagner?

---

[14] http://www.washingtontimes.com/news/2016/jan/21/abraham-wagner-gulen-movement-a-threat-to-us-turke/

# CHAPTER II
# PHILOSOPHY OF SECRECY

# AT FIRST HE DENIES HIS EDUCATOR IDENTITY, AND THEN ACCEPTS IT

Gülen categorially denied allegations about his ties to educational institutions in his statements. He said the same things to *Sabah* and *Hürriyet* newspapers in 1995; and to *Zaman* daily in April 1997. However, in 1998 in *Yeni Yüzyıl* he told Hulusi Turgut: "I always encouraged [the establishment of private schools] and I will continue to do so. If they are transferred to the state, in case permission is given for the establishment of new private schools, I will continue to encourage my friends, and tell them to establish private schools." [1] It is very obvious that Gülen contradicts himself. In the same interview, Gülen also has a salient statement. About the debates on continuous eight-year education, he says "Upon request, he is ready to hand over the private schools he has abroad to the state," [2] in order to protect his schools. He does not make clear how he is ready to hand over the schools abroad which he claims he does not own and has no connections to. [3] It did not occur to Journalist Turgut to pose this question to his respondent.

---

[1] Hulusi Turgut, *Yeni Yüzyıl*, January-February 3, 1998.
[2] Faik Bulut, *Kim Bu Fethullah Gülen*, Berfin Yayınları, Istanbul 2016, p. 227
[3] Fetullah Gülen, in his interview with Nuriye Akman, said, "We should also have a counter strategy against Western missionary activities." *Sabah* newspaper, January, 28 1995.

It is necessary to underline one detail on Gülen's close interest in education. Based on Yavuz Çobanoğlu's scholarly analysis, we can easily say that Gülen sees education as a tool, like other critical issues, for "Taking revenge from the West". According to Çobanoğlu:

*"For Gülen, education is an effort to take revenge from the West..."*

"In Fetullah Gülen's world, education takes the shape of a competition to fight against ignorance. It also provides us with a modern method to cope with the challenges of modern world. Gülen always carries some grudge to take revenge from the West. The main purpose of Gülen's vision is, under the leadership of the new generation, to work and succeed in education and science with the belief born out of this understanding."[4]

Before we return to Gülen's record of testimony, let's check a very important point on the documents he had submitted to the United States Department of Homeland Security Migration Office to acquire a Green Card under the category of "Individuals with extraordinary ability or achievement." Gülen does not feel the necessity to hide his "educator" traits in the report that he sent through his attorneys. His attorneys defended that their client has gained the right to ontain the "extraordinary skilled educator in the field of political and religious studies" visa, and that his works contribute to the US's fight against terrorism".[5] However, the Federal Court's decision is negative based on "Gülen being part of the secularism controversy in Turkey and his domination of 25 billion

---

[4] Yavuz Çobanoğlu, "Fethullah Gülen'in Eğitim ve Ahlâk Anlayışına Eleştirel Bir Bakış", *Eğitim, Bilim, Toplum* Dergisi, Bahar Sayısı, Vol. 6:22 (2008), p. 101.

[5] Nedim Şener, *Ergenekon Belgelerinde Fethullah Gülen ve Cemaat*, Destek Yayınları, Istanbul 2016, p. 57

dollars of economic power which has no clear target".[6] Later Gülen's lawyers appeal to the Pennsylvanian State Court and succeed in getting the permission for residency.[7] Let's continue to read Gülen's statements in official records:

> *"I have no connection to any of the schools in Turkey and abroad..."*

> *"Question:* Did you ever support the toppling of the secular Turkish state in any of your recorded videos?

> *FG:* I did not say anything in that manner because I know that if I did say something like that there would be legal proceedings. I know this for sure as I have been preaching for forty years.

> *Question:* I will repeat the question. Did you ever support the toppling of the secular Turkish state in one of your video recordings, yes or no?

> *FG:* No, never. Definitely no.

---

[6] Razi Canikligil, *ABD Gizli Belgelerinde Fethullah Gülen*, Doğan Kitap, Istanbul 2016.

[7] In 2008, Fetullah Gülen applied to the United States Department of Homeland Security Migration Office for a Green Card under the "Individuals with extraordinary ability or achievement" category. References that were presented were from a wide range of people; retired CIA reporter and director, expert on the Balkans and faculty member at Washington University, George Fidas; former CIA agent, RAND consultant, Graham Fuller; former American Ambasador to Ankara Morton Abramowitz; former Turkish Prime Minister Yıldırım Akbulut; Former Minister of Education, Mehmet Sağlam; TÜGİAD Member of the Board of Directors, Murat Saraylı; Washington Rumi Foundation Director H. Ali Yurtsever; Niagara Foundation President Kemal Öksüz: Some faculty from certain American universities; head of departments and members of Catholic, Jesuit, Evangelist, Greek Orthodox churches. Despite this wide range of support, Gülen's application was denied. His lawyers appealed to the court's decision. The court found the evidence presented inadequate to prove that Gülen fits under the "Individuals with extraordinary ability or achievement" category". State Attorney Patrick L. Meehan said, in reference to Gülen, that "He is a religious and political figure aiming to get academic prestige through paying academics for writing on him and his movement". Gülen appealed the decision. The Court of Appeal provisionally accepted Gülen's Green Card application stating that he is an important religious and political leader and his residency in the States can be in the interest of the US.

*Questions:* Did you ever establish schools in Turkey or elsewhere?

*FG:* I did not establish any school personally.

*Question:* Did anyone else establish schools in Turkey or elsewhere in your name?

*FG:* Not in my name. Not in my name, but they know that I appreciate education and they had my support and encouragement, and I do not know where they established schools.

*Question:* Do you have any connections with the education system in those schools?

*FG:* Absolutely not. I have no connection with this.

*Question:* According to your knowledge, do they teach to overthrow the secular Turkish state in those schools?

*FG:* The Turkish Ministry of Education controls and inspects these schools. So far, they did not find anything of the sort.

*Question:* The question was, do you have knowledge of whether or not students are taught how to overthrow the Turkish secular state in those schools?

*FG:* I do not know those schools. I have never attended them. I have never been there.

Question: Are you Said Nursi's successor?

*FG:* Absolutely not.

*Question:* Do you personally believe that the Turkish secular state needs to be changed?

*FG:* No, I do not believe such a change is necessary."[8]

---

[8] Senem, *Fethullah Gülen'in Konuşmaları ve Pensilvanya İfadesi*, p. 94-95.

Fetullah Gülen states in New Jersey that he wants his legal statements to be sent to the 2$^{nd}$ State Security Court of Ankara to be included in his court file. His legal statement ends with his signing the document in the presence of a public notary. Gülen, denies all the charges in his plea that he sent to the State Security Court.

## He is very sensitive on secrecy

Gülen has been residing in the US since January 1999. Gülen shows his medical reports from the Mayo Clinic stating that he has diabetes, coronary insufficiency and neuropathic arthroplasty causing pain and complications as his reasons for staying in the US and not returning to Turkey. Gülen is very careful in depicting himself as a naive erudite person in official statements, while in the private sphere and closed meetings, he orders his followers to continue to work silently and thoroughly:

> *"Be flexible, travel in their vital veins without coming into prominence..."*

"Do not allow casualty. Instead, work more on what it needs to be done, and how it can be supported. These things should be continuously investigated. In this regard, the protection of our friends is very critical, whether in this circle or the other. As I indicated, in relation to this matter of protection, we can benefit from the aesthetic aspect of things. Be flexible, travel in their vital veins without coming into prominence. In this respect, utilize laws and regulations within the flexibility I just mentioned; outsiders must say that these people are closely obeying the law so that this is what lays behind proper promotions. And this is behind what will bring you to more critical and important positions. That is to say, going further without coming into prominence, without hinting your presence like in these two institutions is very critical. Going further, taking place in their vital positions, and if going back is required, to return without injury and without being exposed are the most important matters."[9]

*"If there is no balance of power, do not use power..."*

"A Muslim does not stop. If you cannot run, then jump. They blocked us in Turkey. We cannot walk. You will create an image of a lake in front of you. You strive hard. Act like you are walking. Because stopping and laziness will bring corrosion. This is what will happen in the judiciary and in civil service. We must walk, if we take the pulse, listen to the heart beat and realize that they will make us to step back, then I will not step back but wait, watch for an opportunity. I mean, everything is a game. It is a game like Kung Fu. It is a game like taekwondo. In other words, it is not always knocking down your opponent with one punch. Sometimes, even escaping your opponent would be a tactical maneuver. If there is no balance of power, do not use power. You will plan exceptionally and walk accordingly. From outside, they will accuse us of cowardice. God will take care of us."[10]

*"Do not make any mistakes or we cannot compensate the defeat..."*

"The whole world is very much afraid of Islamic development, Islamic progress. This heretic, tyrant world cannot tolerate the revival of a people of different race, different thought, different understanding. There is an ob-

---

[9]  Hablemitoğlu, *Köstebek*, p. 25.
[10]  Şener, *Ergenekon Belgelerinde Fethullah Gülen ve Cemaat*, p. 94-96.

ligation to move very cautiously and prudently. The volunteers that would like to serve in this mission accordingly need to act like a diplomat who will govern the world, and after solving the problems in accordance to his plans, he should try to solve it in his country; after solving every problem in his country then what is the world's attitude in this matter? It must be taken into consideration, the last step should not be taken before successfully accomplishing plans in each and every platform. One mistake, will blow it and we cannot compensate for the mistaken defeat. It would be wrong, we cannot compensate. This time they would be the ones to quickly bring us in. They would not allow us recover again. God forbid!..."[11]

After deciphering Gülen's strategic plans, it would be surprising to see the reactions of academics, who wrote articles and books on Fetullah Gülen and his community, and depicted him as a moderate "man of religion" who dedicated his life to Islam.

*"A balanced servant of mission does not say the things he will say immediately. He knows that, if he says everything he needs to say now, there may be some who will not give him the right to live. Conditions may get harsher hence he can end up in a problematical atmosphere."*[12] Gülen's most basic strategy easily effecting his followers is his principle of secrecy that constitutes a philosophical foundation for his critical moves. Gülen, because of his ability on rhetoric and his persuasive skills, can manipulate his followers in any way he likes. Thus, the many local nationals and foreigners from different factions in his circle, may become the means of his strategic aims and his

---

[11] Records of 2nd State Security Court of Ankara, Indictment, August 31, 2001, Dossier no: 2000/124 E.
[12] Private Archive, Desiphered Text. Casette 1, Nuh Mete Yüksel.

power of persuasion. Along with Gülen, his followers are also working in a very wide spectrum of professions ranging from trade to politics, from media to education, and they all act with the same tactical mindset. Gülen, defending that betrayal and lying is legitimate[13] in strategic moves, states in his one sermons:

*"Until we reach our final goal, every way, every method is legitimate..."*

"Until we reach our final goal, every way and every method that takes us to that goal is legitimate. That includes lying and deceiving... You are civilians, you do not have guns and your power lies in the amount of capital you have..."[14] "Whereas in the military, even if you are an individual, along with your personal ability, courage and gun, you could take advantage of your troops, and enslave a general or even an army. Then, those who embrace and plan the future, rather than sit and wait for it, should keep training themselves. When the time comes, he can command his soldiers."[15]

*"We should capture everywhere..."*

"Some friends may think that we need to be heroic to encourage and hearten brave souls. However, since there is no balance of power, I would rather personally prefer to disseminate my system of thought, and conquer and appropriate everything in the name of that system... This is a very important issue for our friends working in the judiciary and civil service institutions. To me, private em-

---

[13] Mubah means permissible. Namely, things that are religiosly permissible, and things that an individual is free to do or not to do.
[14] Gülen, *Fasıldan Fasıla 1*, p. 119.
[15] Erdoğan, *Fethullah Gülen, Küçük Dünyam*, p. 121.

ployees and public servants cannot act in a heroic manner. This would be futile heroism."[16]

*"You will hire judges too..."*

"... Perhaps this is our weakness. I mean, if necessary you are going to turn it all upside down, you are going to take control over it. I tell our friends that we might spend a thousand and get only one back in return. We can expect to raise qualified individuals through our educational institutions... There will be instances where you spend a billion liras, and claim 10 million liras in damages. What is important is to win the case; you will hire lawyers as well as judges..."[17]

*"We are waiting for the Golden Generation..."*

"...Greeks are waiting for someone. They are waiting for a Heraclitus that would save the world from rust and dirt. Christians are awaiting the messiah who will save humanity. The Alawites are waiting for the long-awaited "imam". We are also waiting for something. God willing, we are waiting for the Golden Generation that will conquer everything both inside and outside. To put it more correctly, we are not waiting for the golden generation, we are planning to be the 'Golden Generation'..."[18]

## Chooses his Statements Carefully

Now, let's return to plead no. 2000/124 that Gülen presented to the 2nd State Security Court of Ankara on August 8, 2001. In his plead, we see how his depiction of himself differs from the above-mentioned "provocative" person:

---

[16] Özçelik, *Kâinat İmam Fethullah Gülen*, p. 142.
[17] Ergün Poyraz, *İndeki Vaiz*, Tanyeri Kitap, Istanbul 2014, p. 283.
[18] http://www.sizinti.com.tr/konular/ayrinti/yollari-gozlenen-bir-nesil-bir-ki-tap-nasil-okunmali.html

*"A pious worshipper cannot run after office and status..."*

"You can't judge a person based solely on the one or two things they say. He must be judged by looking at when, to who, why and with what purpose he said what said. So far, I published many books, held sermons and recorded talks. A judgement about me should be reached after taking all these in to consideration. In most of my talks, I declared on many occasions that God's approval is above everything, there is no position higher than serving the faith and Quran. A pious worshipper should have no desire for posts in the state and government. It would not be an exaggeration to say that I repeated this hundreds of times. A pious person needs to enter the hearts of people, endear God to people, and give courage and hope to everyone in the name of spiritual life...

...These days we need tolerance and dialogue more than ever. This is what I do actually. I always wanted be on good terms with everyone and extended my arms to everyone like a brother. Although that merit does not belong to me [but God-given], everyone who knows me would recognize my desire to embrace all. This is a manifestation of my intellectual and spiritual state. For this reason, I desire to meet with everyone. In this spirit, I had met with Turkish ruling political leaders, exchanged opinions and tried to benefit from their experiences. In those meetings, my personal demands, expectations or vested interest in office or status were out of question. The main ideas in all these meetings were the reinforcement of tolerance, dialogue and national reconciliation..."[19]

---

[19]  Records of the 2nd State Security Court of Ankara, Indictment, August 31, 2001, Dossier no: 2000/124 E..

Gülen tries to disprove allegations by depicting himself as a retired man of religion with documents extracted from his earlier articles. This strategy in fact was serving his real goal of *"spinning a spider web with the patience of a spider and waiting for people to fall into it."*[20] Refuting allegations that he infiltrated the Armed Forces, he shows his loyalty to with the following answer:

> *"There are those who would like to present laicite and Atatürkism as irreligiosity..."*

"Never in my life had I done anything contrary to the military, against the military's assents that I would see the military as an obstacle to my activities and would try to infiltrate it. The article titled, "asker yazısı" (soldier's note) that is also published in my book *Çağ ve Nesil* (Age and Generation), which I wrote in 1979, a time when many people pointed guns to the military, is crucial to revealing my thoughts on the military. In reality, by abusing sensitivity of the military on laicite and Atatürkism, those who oppose every manifestation of religion, presenting Atatürkism and laicite as irreligiosity and would like to use it for their own purposes; are trying to provoke the military against this nation's patriotic and pious children... The military intervened in politics on three occasions; in the first occasion, the Chief of Staff was sentenced to life in prison. However, the military never acted against religion or pious people or provoked the military against religion. The real danger is the attempts to pit the military against our nation, from which the military came. I have full confidence that the military is fully aware of this danger."[21]

---

[20] Senem, *Fethullah Gülen'in Konuşmaları ve Pensilvanya İfadesi*, p. 19.
[21] Records of the 2nd State Security Court of Ankara, Defense Statement, August 31, 2001, Dossier no: 2000/124 E .

# CHAPTER III
# DESIRE FOR POWER AND AUTHORITY

.

# HIS DESIRE TO "RUN THE STATE" IS NOTHING NEW

Gülen constructed his plea meticulously and prefers to perplex minds with other questions rather than providing clear answers. We had met with similar tactics of Gülen in his record of statements given to the United States Prosecution Office. Although it is a known fact that setting up Gülenist cadres within the military is of vital importance for Gülen, he tries to acquit himself by expressing his loyalty to the military. As he commands his followers to "live like commandos",[1] he is very careful in hiding his interest in governing the state. Gülen, seemingly a man of religion who has no mission other than showing the people the true path, adopts a very delicate attitude in relation to the government of state mechanisms. Reason being, in Gülen's philosophy, the state is treated as the "reason for existence".[2] It is because of this that Gülen tries to hide through contradictory statements the secret plans that will help him achieve his "noble cause". In this section, let's heed to Yavuz Çobanoğlu's duly analysis of concepts of society, state, morality and authority in Fetullah Gülen:

---

[1] Hikmet Çetinkaya, *Fethullah Gülen'in 40 Yıllık Serüveni*, Cumhuriyet Kitap, Istanbul 2014, p. 50.

[2] M. Hakan Yavuz, "Devlete İnanırım, Devletçi Değilim", Fethullah Gülen interview, *Milliyet*, August 11, 1997.

*"Criticizing the state unfairly should be considered treachery..."*

"In his works Gülen frequently mentions that a nation needs a "supreme state",[3] and the state's mission is to meet this demand... Gülen sees current social cleavages as arbitrary and does not look in favor. He predicts that with a 'new resurrection' all these cleavages will disappear and there will be an overall unification. For this reason, it is impossible to analyze Gülen's idea of state without his ideas on instituting moral and sacred order in the public sphere.

In Islam, the state also has the duty to protect worship, fasting, giving alms and fulfilling other religious duties.[4] For this reason, according to Gülen, the state's oppression of those revolting against the system – even if the system is a democratic and secular one – is a just act.[5] Based on similar reasoning, no harm should come to the state. For this reason, speaking harshly and criticizing the state unjustly, should be considered 'treachery against the nation'".[6]

Gülen, must have forgotten his harsh talks against the government and the state both in the 1970s and recent years that he now allows saying, "Those who unfairly criticize the state are traitors". Gülen does not realize that he positioned himself as a "traitor against the nation", after the failed coup attempt of December 17/25, 2013 orchestrated by Gülen's followers in the Justice Department, aiming to annihilate the legitimate government, and calling the government and

---

[3]   Fethullah Gülen, *Çağ ve Nesil 1*, Nil Yayınları, İzmir 1982, p. 88.
[4]   Doğan Duman, *Demokrasi Sürecinde'de İslamahk*, Dokuz Eylül Publishing, Istanbul 1999, p. 281.
[5]   Fethullah Gülen, *Ümit Burcu (Kırık Testi 4)*, Nil Publishing, İzmir 2005, p. 187.
[6]   Yavuz Çobanoğlu, *Altın Neslin Peşinde*, İletişim Publishing, Istanbul 2012, pp 255-256.

Prime Minister "hyenas, snakes and centipedes".[7] It is clearly understood that Gülen's democratic attitude, like his statism, is nothing but a foundation for his unethical discourse and actions on the path to his "holy mission".

Gülen's passion for "power and authority" has taken a pathological state not only in Turkey but worldwide. It is known that Gülen has a close interest in regional politics and educational institutions in 165 countries.[8] It is crucial to understand the point Gülen's power has reached in Balkan countries. For example, people were appointed to Religious Affairs Offices in some countries after consulting with Pennsylvania.[9] It may be thought that the complaisance for Gülen in the Balkans is due to his identity as a man of religion. However, Gülen's idea of "the ends justify the means", is surely a religious deviation. Let's look at the observations of Professor Hakan Yavuz who closely follows the Gülen Movement's activities abroad, on Gülen's *"break from Risale-i Nur"*:

*"It is wrong to call the Gülen Movement a 'Nurcu' movement..."*

"The Gülen Movement was inspired by the *Risale-i Nur* movement. However the movement is not in the same place as it started. That is to say, the Gülen Movement had different periods. First, it had a *dadaş* period. There used to be an Islam blended with nationalism that was, with the impact of the Cold War, seen in anti-communism associations, that saw Islam as a toold against communism and said, "silence these leftists". After the 1980s, there is a Gülen Movement that would like to keep up with neoliberal economic policies. However, it is not appropriate to call the Gülen Movement a "Nurcu movement". At that

---

[7] http://herkul.org/herkul-nagme/402-nagme-birlik-dirlik-ve-beraberligin-yolu/
[8] Ankara Public Prosecutor's Office, Fethullah Gülen Indictment no. 2000/420.
[9] http://www.milliyet.com.tr/balkanlar-daki-feto-dunya-2285462/

point in time in the Gülen Movement, power and governance gained supremacy. Being powerful, and holding governance became values themselves...

...The Gülen Movement became a movement that was shaped by a leader. Maybe Gülen realized this change and interpreted Islam in a Calvinist fashion. With or without coincidence, he integrated in the global system, and became quite "successful". However, this success was temporary. As the Gülen Movement became integrated in the capitalist system, capitalism was integrated in them too. That is to say, Calvinism [10] started with good intentions, but later it turned in to a dictatorship, and then collapsed. It had a serious decline. The movement is winning the world while losing Islam. In other words, the moral dimension of Islam was pushed to the background. It was bounded to power. It reached a point where the ends justified the means. And they surrendered to modernity.

*"The Gülen Movement is a practice-oriented movement, with the goal of seizing power..."*

In my opinion, he should have criticized modernity. Instead the movement succumbed to economy. The spirit of capitalism dominated religious rationality. Capitalism redefined religious values. For this reason, the Gülen Movement gained an important Calvinist dimension. The movement infiltrated Turkey in all corners. Today, the movement has temporary success only, there is no desire, vision or intellectual erudition to create a change in the movement. Because it is a practical movement that aims to

---

[10] Calvinism is a Christian denomination, founded by Jean Calvin in the sixteenth century. It advocated the establishment of social institutions based not on traditional values but fundementalist Christian principles. Calvinists, by providing rational and scientific education to their members, paved the way to the development of science and technology.

capture state apparatuses. The Gülen Movement is trying to prove that the United States is on their side. There is no such thing. The United States does not need the movement. The movement needs the US. You know Gülen's Green Card process... What happened is that the US is using Gülen to influence the Turkish military..."[11]

Ruşen Çakır, an expert on Islamic movements in Turkey, claims that Gülen and his community are educating people with "agitation and speculative arguments"[12] with the aim of *"ruling the state"*:

"The members of the Gülen Movement are one of the most insistent and successful defendants of the popular Islamic thought of adopting the West's science but keeping the tradition intact. They targeted young people at school age, and raised many "brave fellows" as a result of their mission. Their cadres are asked to be at the service of the state (at least for the time being). The movement has huge financial backing. It can be "theoretically" assumed that, one day, when the community has self-confidence, it may develop a desire to run the state. However, it is not clear for how much longer this cadre, which is raised with agitated and speculative arguments, and developed around a person-cult, can move along..."[13]

## His interest in intelligence

Fetullah Gülen, who spent a considerable amount of time thinking on the concepts of state and authority, has sugges-

---

[11] Serdar Akinan, "A conversation with Prof. Hakan Yavuz", *SkyTürk*, July 2008. http://arsiv.gercekgundem.com/?p=144531

[12] Ruşen Çakır, *Ayet ve Slogan*, Metis Yayınları, Istanbul 1990, p. 118.

[13] Ruşen Çakır, *Ayet ve Slogan*, p. 119.

tions for his followers on issues like "intelligence and information gathering."[14] It seems that Gülen has a deep interest in intelligence. In one his books, he advises his followers as follows:

> "On the one hand, we should know the enemy on inside with the help of our perfectly-running intelligence services; and on the other hand, we should not let our enemy to reside among us to gather information. Yes, we should concentrate on each dynamic that is important for the perpetuity of the state and nation. We need to systematize these dynamics, and taking advantage of technology, we should carry out our activities. Especially on gathering intelligence, we should be very much ahead of our enemy...."[15]

At first glance, Gülen's advices may not be understood clearly. Or they can be found confusing. Gülen felt the need to make a statement on the Gazi Mahallesi events that took place in Istanbul in 1995. In this statement, he unintentionally deciphered a very interesting detail. This detail is almost the embodiment of his above mentioned abstract advices. Let's read the statements in which Gülen confessed that he knew about the Gazi Mahallesi events before they happened: [16]

*"I knew about the Gazi Mahallesi events 1.5 months before they happened..."*

"...I am not sure whether I am supposed to be saying this, but based on some intelligence reports, I would like say few

[14] Selim Çoraklı, *Darbelerin Efendisi Hocia*, Publishing, Istanbul 2016, p. 34.
[15] Gülen, *Fasıldan Fasıla 1*, p. 113-114.
[16] Gazi Mahallesi events: Events that started on March 12, 1995, after an attack on civilians in a coffee house occupied mainly by the Alawites. The event spread throughout the city. As a result of the spread of violence that lasted until March 1995, 22 people had lost their lives, and hundreds have been wounded, or arrested.

things on a certain issue. Will you allow me pragmatism here? In this matter, only men who devote their life to a certain cause can be arrogant. I am not a good man. One-and-a-half months before the Gaziosmanpaşa events, I had informed one of the closest people to the head of the state that there will be bomb explosions throughout Turkey. I said that there were some plans on Turkey, read the report that was given to me by a friend. Someone wants to trick the Alawites. Some Alawites will arson various places. There are some journals in Europe devoted to his issue. I had given the 20-30-page report a month and a half before the events happened. They will target some Alawite places and then say the Sunnis targeted the Alawites; then the Alawites will revolt. I submitted the report and waited to see if the rulers could find a solution. Then I realized that I had made a mistake. For example, that report could have been given to the media. The report could be discussed on Samanyolu TV, for example, by the *Ayna* program, as I know the producer personally."[17]

During the event in which 22 people had died, Süleyman Demirel was the President and Tansu Çiller was the Prime Minister. In Gülen's gory confession, it is hard to understand who he meant by the "head of state". Gülen's relations with intelligence and his success in getting "intelligence" becomes more frightening when we consider that the reasons behind the Gazi Mahallesi events are yet to be clarified.

We see that it is habitual for Gülen to make a statement after important events in Turkey and abroad. In 2005, as he makes another statement on the current agenda, he warns his followers and authorities about "The need for intelligence services that need to work more diligently."[18]

---

[17] www.f-gulen.org.
[18] Çoraklı, *Darbelerin Efendisi Hocia*, p. 148.

*"Intelligence services would have everything under control if they wanted..."*

"If three or four people take to the streets, the others will follow them, wondering what had happened there. For this reason, intelligence services need to be on alert to prevent this problem. I believe that if police, JİTEM (Gendarmerie Intelligence and Counterterrorism) and the National Intelligence Services want, they can control everything in Turkey. I, as a citizen, personally resent this. If something happens without their consent, it means that they were not doing their job. Their situation needs to be reconsidered. However, I am aware of their hyper sensitivity on other matters. For example, they investigate what so and so had for lunch, what he prepares for dinner, or what he will eat at breakfast. If they know all this, but do not know the things that would drag Turkey into chaos, then I would think that they pretend not to know them. I feel that by the grace of God, if they are a little patient, they can eliminate the source of sedition and disorder. That is what concerns us...."[19]

## Why is intelligence so important?

To grasp the importance of intelligence for Gülen, let's take a look at former Chief of Police Intelligence Bureau Hanefi Avcı's book titled *Haliç'te Yaşayan Simonlar*. Avcı reveals why the Intelligence Bureau and KOM (Bureau of anti-smuggling and Organized Crimes) are vitally important for the Gülen "community" as follows:

"The first thing they do is capture and control the Police Intelligence Bureau, in order to collect information

[19]  http://www.haber7.com/haber.php?haber_id=121422

as they please throughout the country and to follow the activities of some certain people. They need to dominate the bureau. They can do it through dominating the National Intelligence Organization (MİT) as well, but that institution would not allow them to move further. If they have intentions other than simply collecting information on people and institutions and if they would like to start a judicial process, then they are obliged to dominate KOM. It is not enough to be active at the center of the bureau but also need to capture branches in major cities such as Istanbul and Ankara. If collecting information on people and institutions and starting a judicial process are not enough and they want to take legal action on civil servants, soldiers and anyone who is protected under certain laws, then they would need to have strong influence on judges and prosecutors of courts. Police Intelliegence Bureau Directorate, with its state-of-the-art technology, can collect any type of information on anyone, discover who is meeting with whom, and ascertain connections and relations of anyone who uses a telephone. Nobody can hide their connections and relations from them.

Police Intelligence Bureau Directorate with all its branches in the cities and even in some small towns, have the authority to listen. People are listened to, watched, and after some time, documents are destroyed. There are information banks for more than terabytes on each and every institution and matter that are collected over years. Moreover, having branches in every city in Turkey equipped with unimaginable technical equipment, through employing 7,000 personnel, the institution can surveilance the entire country. They can only be inspected by the Interior Ministry and Chief Police Constable; nobody can enter their buildings, meddle in their business, including the inspectors.

KOM's head of department generally investigates organized crime and groups throughout the country. At the same time, it is the most efficient center of the police force on listening and surveillance. Special Court judges and prosecutors, by pushing some laws, can sue, take into custody and arrest anyone. However, under normal conditions, investigation of crimes of civil servants can only be done by certain offices under the law no. 4483. Town clerks are supposed to get permission for anything they do. Likewise, city officials are supposed to get permission from the governors, and academics are supposed to get permission from the rector or the Higher Education Board (YÖK). Without these authorizations, no legal action can be taken, apart from some cases of being caught in the act, prosecutors cannot carry out any investigations. However if it is claimed that any act is under the jurisdiction of Special Courts, anyone can be sued.

Lately, we see that such a plan is in action in Turkey. If you control the MİT, then you can solely collect intelligence; you may distort and use them but you do not take any further action. If you want to take any further action, the MİT will not be enough. In this regard, we can obviously understand today that some people at KOM headquarters, the Directorate of Intelligence, Intelligence Departments in Ankara and Istanbul, and in all branches of judiciary are composed of people with certain tendencies."[20]

---

[20] Hanefi Avcı, *Haliç'te Yaşayan Simonlar, Dün Devlet Bugün Cemaat,* Angora Publishing, Ankara 2010, pp 416-418.

## According to FBI Adviser Williams, Gülen is a "sick Turkish preacher"

Let's give a break to Gülen's interest in intelligence and take a look at what another intelligence officer says on Gülen. Former FBI adviser, current faculty of Wilkes University, Professor Paul Williams, describes Gülen as *"the most dangerous Islamist alive"*.[21] In his article published in a local Pennsylvanian newspaper, *Pocono Record*, in 2010, he says Gülen is a *"sick Turkish preacher"* with an armed organization.

*"Gülen: The world's most dangerous Islamist..."*

"Do not seek the world's most dangerous Islamist in Afghanistan, Pakistan, Sudan or in Somalia. With his $30-billion, right under our noses, he is trying to establish a worldwide caliphate. Military training is provided at the camp with AK-47s. People living in areas around the camp make complaints to the FBI about the gun noises. The FBI raided here many times. However, they achieved no concrete results. At the 28-acre ranch, helicopters fly low and disturb every one. How do the CIA, FBI and the government remain silent about the activities of Gülen living in this ranch, which is protected like a castle by 100 armed men....?"[22]

We are not sure whether William's allegations are true or not. We do not have enough evidence to know the accuracy of the claims. When Williams's article made tremendous impact on the public, Gülen's attorney started to take action against those claims. However, we see that Williams does not give in and writes another article in the following

---

[21] http://freedomoutpost.com/worlds-most-dangerous-islamist-alive-well-and-living-in-pennsylvania/
[22] Canikligil, *Amerikan Gizli Belgelerinde Fethullah Gülen*, p. 30.

month. This time with a better documented text, he claimed that Gülen was financed by the CIA. Another striking detail is the differing attitudes of the CIA and FBI towards Gülen. In his second article Williams writes:

*"Does the CIA meet the needs of an Islamist...?"*

"Fetullah Gülen, the so-called most dangerous Islamist in the world, obtained permanent residency (Green Card). Now he can reside in his mansion in Pennsylvania for the rest of his life, thanks to former CIA agent Graham Fuller and American Foreign Service officers. Fuller sent a letter of recommendation to the federal judge in Pennsylvania, in support of Fetullah Gülen's Green Card application. The former CIA agent stated that Gülen deserves to reside and be protected in the US as he is an "Individual with extraordinary ability". However, Gülen is not even a high school graduate. Well, then why did Fuller support an immigrant who fled Turkey with the intention of toppling the government and establishing a New Islamist World Order through sedition? The answer to this question comes from various documents and researcher Sibel Edmonds.

*"CIA financed him..."*

The CIA financed Gülen with money it acquired from drug trafficking. Gülen is supported to gain control over Central Asia through agents graduated from Gülen-affiliated schools in the region. Gülen established radical madrasahs and communities in Uzbekistan, Azerbaijan, Kazakhstan, Turkmenistan and other newly established former Russian states to control gas and petroleum reserves...

...Starting from 1999, the CIA supported Gülen's efforts to overthrow Turkey's secular government to control the newly established countries in Central Asia, and establish a solid base in the region. As Turkish officials understood Gülen's intentions, they pressed charges of sedition against Gülen. Upon this, he fled from Turkey to the US with the special immigration status of "minister of religion."[23]

[23] https://counterjihadreport.com/2013/08/30/more-dangerous-than-bin-laden-protestors-to-descend-on-gulens-mountain-fortress-in-pennsylvania/

# CHAPTER IV
## INSTRUMENTALITY OF "TOLERANCE"

# GÜLEN'S ANTI-SEMITIC RHETORIC

The thoughts of Gülen, who holds the international patent for interreligious dialogue, on different belief systems, are concrete evidence to understanding the working mechanisms of his "strategic intelligence". Gülen, whose rhetoric on Jews can be indeed regarded as "hate speech", had met with the Catholic world's spiritual leader John Paul II at the end of the 1990s and prepared for the establishment of a joint university at which all three religions curriculums will be included. Let's read his statements on Jews, describing them as a servile tribe:

*"The Jewish tribe is miserable ..."*

"...Jews preserved their racial characteristics despite having scattered around the world and living an almost nomadic life without a nation for centuries. The Jewish tribe is intelligent. Throughout history, this intelligent tribe made many discoveries in science and philosophy. However, they always presented it to the world as poisonous honey. For example, Karl Max is a Jew, and his theory of communism may be seen as a viable alternative to capitalism, however, it is a deadly poison mixed with honey... Jews will protect their identity until doomsday. When we approach doomsday, their duty to serve as an obstacle against the development of humanity will come to an end, and they will prepare their own end. Leave aside their hostility towards Islam and Muslims; the tribe that disdained its own prophet and slaughtered many will be like Nazis and will search for places to hide all over the world. Nevertheless, I will spare the details of the reason behind this issue, as it would create unnecessary excitement. It seems that until Islam is able to find its place, the future will continue to belong to the Jews for a while...."[1]

There is contradiction between Gülen's anti-Semitic rhetoric and his statement on the Mavi Marmara incident. The Mavi Marmara flotilla loaded with humanitarian aid en route to Gaza, was attacked by Israeli soldiers in international waters. Gülen called those onboard the flotilla rebels as "they did not obtain permission from the authorities".[2] Here it is very interesting to see that Gülen, although he personally loathes Jews, refers to Israel as the legitimate authority. Another striking detail is where Gülen was residing at the time he made these paradoxical statements. One other important detail is that it was former American ambassador to Turkey, Morton Abramowitz, a Jew, who helped Gülen establish a school in Israel and connections with Jewish lobbies.[3] One wonders why Jewish lobbies, which are quite sensitive about anti-Semitism, would support the insincere and paradoxical Gülen, and help the development of the Gülen community.

## He steps back

After his anti-Semitic statements were published in *The Atlantic* journal in 2013, he gave another interview to the same journal.

---

[1] Gülen, *Fasıldan Fasıla 1*, p. 15.
[2] http://www.ntv.com.tr/dunya/fethullah-gulen-israilden-izin-almaliydilar,kIC_HTknIEavwlzh-VOxdg
[3] Bulut, *Kim Bu Fethullah Gülen*, p. 164.

There, Gülen admits, *"There was a time when I once misinterpreted Quranic verses"*[4] and used false rhetoric against Jews. In fact Gülen confesses that *"He also criticized the terrorists and suicide bombers"*:

### *"I had misinterpreted Quranic verses on Jews..."*

"It is possible to analyze this matter from different perspectives. It is very normal to see that one can change his mind. In one of my articles I tried to explain that nobody is the same person they were yesterday. Your interlocutors change too. Even though you may be the same person today, this does not mean that you or your interlocutors will remain the same tomorrow. Through the interreligious dialogue initiative we started in the 1990s, I had the opportunity to learn about the different faiths. This knowledge, thus, requires a change in my previous statements. I need to sincerely confess that I misinterpreted verses and hadiths on Jews and I might have been wrong in my explanations. I realized that, the criticism and damnation of Jews in the Quran and Sunnah do not target a certain belief or group of people holding that belief, but criticism is based on characteristics that any human being may have. I also know that some of my ideas were taken out of context and misused by various people. I had certain criticisms concerning some of Israel's conducts, yet, during my sermons at the mosque I criticize terrorism and suicide bombings that target innocent people as well."[5]

## His Supporters: Jesuit Priest Thomas Michel and Michael Rubin

Let's take a break from Gülen's contradictory statements and look at articles written in 2005 by Thomas Michel, a Jesuit

---

4   Süleyman Yeşilyurt, *Pensilvanya Canbazı*, Alter Publishing, Istanbul 2014, p. 165.
5   http://www.theatlantic.com/international/archive/2013/08/a-rare-meeting-with-reclusive-turkish-spiritual-leader-fethullah-gulen/278662/

priest and Georgetown University faculty, who helped Gülen reside in Pennsylvania with his reference:

> "These people are openly modern people. They are well educated in the sciences. They have sincere concerns about human and moral values. They want to pass on their knowledge to students through their demeanor. They provide first class education through state-of-the-art technology, character formation and high ideals. To me, Gülen schools are the most efficient proof of his efforts to create harmony between modernity and moral values. This is one of the most striking and promising educational entrepreneurship in the whole world."[6]

As understood from Michel's writings, Gülen's supporters are not only Jewish scientists and politicians. Important figures from the Jesuit world are also competing against one another to give their support to Gülen. After the failed July 15 coup attempt, to defend Gülen, Michel who lauds Gülen and his schools, wrote an article in the *Common Weal* against President Recep Tayyip Erdoğan that disregards all codes of civility.[7] His statements imply more than what they say. It is important to understand the level of loyalty and respect that Rubin has for Gülen. However, where his boldness comes from, is unknown. It is sufficient, for the time being, to note that the article was published in a Catholic journal and the Vatican chooses to keep silent on the matter.

## An Article of Regret from Rubin

It is not difficult to guess the kind of relationship Gülen has

---

[6]   Thomas Michel, S.J., "Sufism and Modernity in the Thought of Fethullah Gülen", *The Muslim World*, Special Issue, July 2005, Vol. 95, No: 3, p. 341-358.
[7]   https://www.commonwealmagazine.org/why-turkey-targeting-hizmet

with Thomas Michel. It is curious why people like Thomas Michel risk their career in order to protect Gülen and his community. It is hence not surprising to see a radical change in the opinions of certain people affiliated with the FBI and CIA, who were formerly bitter of critics of Gülen and his supporters. One does not need to be genius to discover the codes of this change. Personal and human weaknesses would enlighten us about the nature of this change. Once the most formidable opponents of Gülen, a researcher at the American Enterprise Institute, Michael Rubin, writes in *National Review* in 2008 that *Gülen was a very dangerous follower of Sharia that he was making plans to topple the government, and return to Turkey like Khomeini.* He defines Gülen as *"A very dangerous man and his community that run billions of dollars of funds, active in a wide spectrum, from media to education, trade, politics, culture and arts. He tries to place millions of his followers in the Justice Department and Ministry of Interior."*[8] Seven years later, in his 2015 article titled, *"Re-evaluation of Fetullah Gülen,"* he openly apologizes to Gülen:

> *"I apologize from Gülen and his supporters..."*

> Fetullah Gülen, the 74-year-old Turkish Islamic thinker, has long been the subject of controversy in both American and Turkish policy circles. Born in Erzurum, Turkey, he taught and preached in Turkey for decades. His writings have focused on the interplay between religion, modernism, and interfaith tolerance, though his critics have suggested that his public and private statements were often at odds with each other. He came to the United States in 1999 seeking medical treatment for diabetes, among other ailments. While in the United States, vid-

---

[8] http://www.nationalreview.com/article/224182/turkeys-turning-point-michael-rubin

eotapes surfaced which apparently showed Gülen suggesting his goal was to change Turkey's system to make it more religious. Gülen and his supporters say the tapes were manipulated and his remarks twisted and taken out of context, but others suspected a wolf in sheep's clothing. Gülen chose to stay in the United States rather than face prosecution in Turkey. After all, then as now justice was not the highest priority for the Turkish judicial system. He has since lived in Pennsylvania, near the Poconos town of Saylorsburg....Back in 2009, the *Middle East Quarterly*, a policy journal which I used to edit, published an article by Turkey expert and translator Rachel Sharon-Krespin about Gülen. The article ascribed malevolent motives to Gülen's work. John Esposito, director of the Prince Alwaleed Center for Muslim–Christian Understanding at Georgetown University, in contrast, embraces Gülen's work and teachings and affirmed his sincerity...In my own writing, I have often been suspicious of the Gülen movement, although as I reflect, I realize I may have been misread the movement.

Was I right to be suspicious of the (sic) Fetullah Gülen and his movement? To some extent, yes. But was I at times unfair to the group? Absolutely. I regret that I once speculated that Gülen's return to Turkey could mirror Khomeini's return to Tehran, a comparison which became headline news in the often polemical Turkish press. Indeed, for that comparison, I apologize. Would I want to be judged by the same standards by which I judged the movement? Probably not. Does that mean I endorse the movement? No, I do not. But I am willing to listen to them. [9]

---

[9]  https://www.commentarymagazine.com/foreign-policy/middle-east/reconsidering-fethullah-gulen/

## Gülen also targets the Vatican

Fetullah Gülen, meeting with the spiritual leader of the Catholic world and head of the state of the Vatican, Pope John Paul II in 1998, as an ordinary man of religion, made a move to start interfaith dialogue. It is hard to understand why the Vatican chose to collaborate with a retired preacher instead of the Turkish Presidency of Religious Affairs which has a huge organization abroad. However, the fact that former CIA-affiliated Americans and Jews prepared the foundation of interfaith dialogue indicates that Gülen's network of relations is much more complex than it is thought. At this point, we see that Graham Fuller, who was a former CIA Chief of Operation in Turkey and the Middle East, started to be an avid supporter of the Gülen Movement. Before getting into the details of the historic letter he presented to the Vatican and his meeting with Pope John Paul II, let's look at Gülen's thoughts on the Vatican:

*"Vatican is behind all the bloodshed in the Islamic world..."*

"The missionary organization is behind all of the atrocities in the world. The Vatican is behind it. It is a centipede nest, a cobra nest. The Vatican is behind the bloodshed in Sarajevo. The Vatican is behind the bloodshed in Kashmir. They have lobbies in the United States. If a Christian organization is slightly aggravated, all hell will break loose. I mean they would make a huge scene. They write letters. I wish such things do not happen there, as they are also our brothers. This is another issue. All this is happening in different parts of the world, from Kashmir to Palestine, to Somalia. They are looking for opportunities to invade Sudan. They keep their silence about the bloodshed in Palestine..."[10]

---

[10] Nuh Mete Yüksel, Chief Public Prosecutor of State Security Court, Private

"Today, together with the world, we see once again, the Vatican's great lie. While no help was sent to Bosnia-Herzegovina, the Croatian border is protected with 14,000 UN soldiers. They do not talk about the Muslims murdered in Bosnia-Herzegovina. However, they have no problems with war orphans being kidnapped to try and evangelize them!! I wish all these happenings would wake up Muslims and trigger them to strive for their religion and people."[11]

Although he made several negative statements about the Vatican and the Catholic world, a world of which Jesuit Priest Thomas Michel is a part, Gülen had a 30-minute meeting with Pope John Paul II. The meeting was followed enthusiastically by both Turkish and Western media. Gülen took the most strategic step that will help him gain international popularity. It is still unclear why the Catholic world gave credit to "the plan to save the universe" and Gülen's attempt to make himself visible in the international arena. Gülen's meeting with the Pope had been criticized by the Islamic segment of the society in Turkey. Despite harsh criticism, Gülen did not step back. The debate was ignited when letter Gülen presented to Pope John Paul II was leaked to the media. Let's remember the letter that proposed to find a common ground for the three Abrahamic religions to show Gülen's faith and brightness.

### "His Holiness the Pope.

We brought you greetings from the people of the Holy Land where the three religions were born. They were the people who were cognizant of our holy mission to trans-

---

Archieve recordings, no. 14.

[11] Fethullah Gülen, *Prizma 1*, Nil Publishing, 3rd edition, İzmir 1996, p. 226.

form this world into a livable habitat. We present our most sincere thanks to you as you spare time for us in your busy schedule, and grant us the pleasure to meet with you.

We are here to be a part of the Papacy Council for Interfaith Dialogue (PCID) that was started and continued by his Holiness the Pope Paul VI. We would like to see the realization of this mission. We came to you, in the most humble manner and even with daring, to present our humble help to your most precious mission.

Islam is a misunderstood religion. In fact it is Muslims who must be accused most for this misunderstanding. An effort at the right time in the right place may contribute to diminishing this misunderstanding. The Muslim world will welcome an opportunity that will eliminate this misunderstanding with open arms.

Humanity has, from time to time denied science for religion or denied religion for science, as they think they have contradicting natures. All knowledge belongs to Allah and religion comes from Allah. In that case, how can the two be contradicting? Our joint efforts to increase tolerance and understanding between people through interfaith dialogue may function very well. In our country, we were in dialogue with various Christian sects. We would like to express that these efforts were not futile. Our aim is to institute brotherhood among the three religions through tolerance and understanding. We can together take a stance against those who lost their way, those want to see the clash of civilizations, those who are skeptical like jetty or a barrier if you will.

Last year, we had organized an international symposium with the concept of interfaith dialogue in collaboration with internationally-known scientists. We would like to repeat such activities after the success of our endeavor. For the time being, we are in the process of organizing a conference on interfaith dialogue in hopes that the Vatican will be represented.

We do not claim that we have new ideas. We would like to present some proposal to closely serve your mission. We would like to propose some joint activities, including visits to certain sacred places in the Middle East like Antioch, Tarsus, Ephesus and Jerusalem, to mark the third millennium of Christianity. We take this as an opportunity to repeat our President Demirel's invitation to you to visit our country and as well as the holy sites.

The people of Anatolia are waiting enthusiastically to welcome you and show you their hospitality. Through establishing dialogue with Palestinian leaders, we can pave the way to joint visits to Jerusalem. This visit may be a giant step towards declaring this holy city an international zone that can be visited by Christians, Jews and Muslims without any restriction – or even without any visa requirements.

We propose to organize a series of conferences to be held in major capital cities, starting from Washington, D.C., with the collaboration of the religious leaders of the three major religions. For the timing of the second series, the 2,000th birthday of Prophet Jesus can be ideal.

A student exchange program will be very beneficial. Educating pious young people together will strengthen their unity. Within the framework of the exchange program, a seminary school can be established in Urfa, where the father of all three religions, Prophet Abraham was born.

This could be put to practice by either expanding existing programs at Harran University, or by establishing an independent university that would have a comprehensive curriculum, meeting the needs of the three religions. The proposed programs may be regarded as big projects, however, they are not undoable. There are two kinds of people in the world. Some try to adapt themselves to the society, while others, rather than adapting to society, want to impose their own values to the society. Society owes all the developments to the latter. Thank God for creating them. (M. Fetullah Gülen / A Humble Servant of God / February 9, 1998)"[12]

## His mind is full of controversies about Alawism

Fetullah Gülen, who uses every opportunity to declare he has tolerance toward different faiths, does not, for some reason, have the same tolerance toward Alawism, which is considered one of the spiritual traditions in Islam. [13] In one private home meeting, Gülen shares his thoughts on Alawism: "The most dangerous movement in Turkey, a hundred times more dangerous than the PKK, is Alawism..."[14] He additionally accuses Alawites of being extremists[15] and refers to Muawiya's son, Yazid, as "our":

"I am fascinated when I look at Allah's work. There was devil worshipping in Yazidism. However, this matter originated from our famous Yazid. This Yazid, to say so in colloquial language, was so ugly. Yazid emerged from

---

[12] Bulut, *Kim Bu Fetullah Gülen*, p. 272 -274.
[13] http://www.cnnturk.com/2012/turkiye/10/07/diyanet.isleri.baskanindan.alevil-ik.aciklamasi/679605.0/index.html
[14] Poyraz, *İhanet ve Darbe*, p. 229.
[15] Extremist: exceeding the ordinary, usual, or expected. See the TDK for details.

among the Alawites. It is the Alawites who created him... He was a man of reaction.

Upon seeing some of his good acts, people started to look at him in a positive light. For example, whenever we said Yazid, they said, "may God destroy him and curse him". He has good sides too. I am telling you. He became the caliph after his father Mu'awiyyah. He conquered Africa. Those who see his good sides are grateful.

However, the extremist Alawites refuse to accept any of his virtues. For them, Ali, Hassan and Hussein were the only virtuous people. Without saying Ali, Hassan, Hussein, this conquest would be futile even if you conquered Africa or Europe... This is an extreme way of thinking..."[16]

Throughout time, Gülen realizes important contradictions in his thoughts on Alawism. It is understood that, especially in the first years that he began to reside in the States, he tries to infiltrate the Alawites by proposing his mosque-cemevi projects to Alawite associations. Despite everything, Gülen's view on Alawites continues to remain problematic. Gülen goes as far as claiming that he himself is an Alawite in an interview with Ruşen Çakır after the 1995 Gazi Mahallesi incidents:

*"I can easily place my head under Alawites' feet..."*

"In the household I was born and raised, at the madrasa, the lodge where I was educated, and in the line with Bediüzzaman's ideology; the love of "the Prophet's household" and the love of Alawite mysticism were one of the main components. Because of the love of "the Prophet's household, Ahl al-Bayt", my passion for Ali overshadows

---

[16] Poyraz, İhanet ve Darbe, pp 230-231.

the love of other companions. We open our heart to the Alawites who say they love Ali, Fatimah, Hassan and Hussein. We have this very profound side that is open to everyone. We can easily say that we are ready to help any Alawite at any level. I can easily put my head under their feet. In this regard, because of the Gaziosmanpaşa incidents I said, "I am an Alawite". My mother was just as much an Alawite. My father was just as much an Alawite. Because it was my father who inseminated this feeling and this thought in me. Yes, he was the one who inspired the idea of heroism in my heart by telling stories on Ali's heroism..."[17]

Despite all efforts on the part of the movement to approach Alawites, they prefer to remain distanced. In a BBC interview in 2014, Gülen says that his mosque-cemevi project was protested by the Alawites. He makes self-criticism and clarifies accusations on "Alawism without Ali":[18]

"There are important Alawite figures in Turkey like Professor İzzettin Doğan. We had met with previously. I went to visit him at his house and he came to ours. We thought that this issue might constitute a problem. We believed that this was very important for the unity and togetherness of Alawites in Turkey. We may be wrong, everyone can be wrong from time to time. However, most of the Alawites expressed their support of the idea. Some mentioned their concern with regards to the matter of assimilation. Among those who expressed this, there were those who did not recognize Ali. They are called Alawites without Ali. To them, 'Ali is a symbolic hero, a reb-

---

[17] http://rusencakir.com/Fethullah-Gulen-Butun-Alevilerin-ayaklarinin-altina-basimi-rahatlikla-koyabilirim/2065
[18] Ruşen Çakır, Semih Sakallı, *Yüz Soruda Erdoğan x Gülen Savaşı*, Metis Publishing, Istanbul 2014, p. 133.

el in some matters, and should be appreciated for his attitude. However, Ali was a Muslim. Those who were not concerned with matters like Ali's religious thinking, opposed the project. I believe one day they will regret this. The mosque-cemevi project was not planned with the intention of one side assimilating the other."[19]

## His Dilemmas on Women

Gülen's view on women holds serious problems as well. In several of his talks, he said, "[He] did not get married because he had a dream about it, and he also did not want his movement (hizmet) to be interrupted."[20] His opinion on women is not only problematic but also frivolous. Gülen has good dialogues with some Western female academics, journalists and politicians. It can be said that Gülen's opinions on women are based on misinterpretations of traditional Islamic sources. Before getting into the writings of Gülen, let's have a look at one of his talks from 2008:

> "Satan came to the presence of Allah. He said, "You disgraced me, You took everything away from me. Give me one gift, with which I will deviate your servants". Allah said "Let me give you a fortune". Satan did not want it. "Let me give you fame". He refused. Allah said, "Let me give you this, that…" Satan shrugged his shoulders like a child and refused. Then Allah said, "Let me give you the

---

[19] www.bbc.co.uk/turkce/haberler/2014/01/140126_fethullah_gulen_roportaj_guney.shtml

[20] Erdoğan, *Fethullah Gülen, Küçük Dünyam*, pp 64-65. "For a while, I thought of getting married. It was an empherremal idea. The next day a friend of mine came early in the morning and told me this: Last night, I dreamed of our master, the Prophet. He sent his greetings to you and said, 'On the day he got married he will die and I will not attend to his funeral'. It was just a dream. I also know one can not act based on dreams, however, I tried to be respectful to this sign."

ability to exploit." Satan gladly leaped at the opportunity and danced with joy. These are the things with which Hell is surrounded."[21]

We do not know why Gülen shared this anecdote, although it is not supported by any authentic Islamic sources. Since it is not in the scope of this book to analyze Gülen's religious belief, let's continue to read his statements on women:

*"I look in favor of people saying women are not clever enough..."*

"The place where women have the upper hand over men is in the bedroom. If a woman dominates the man there, the man cannot dominate women in other segments of life. If men manage to escape defeat in the bedroom by giving women what they want, and preserve privacy and without transgressing moral borders, then it would be easy to discipline women at the psychological level..."[22]

"Now, let me ask you: which rational man can object to beating a woman if she transgresses? If one out of every 100 women can be disciplined by beating, then why would Islam be against it...?"[23] "Our forefathers say the needle in the hand of a woman is like a spear in the hands of the mujahideen. When I see women who became slaves of their desires, I look in favor of people who say women are not clever..."[24]

There is no way Gülen's twisted thought on women could be accepted by the society. It is important to see the level of culture of obedience "in the community" by looking at "sis-

[21] http://odatv.com/kadinlar-cehennemin-etrafini-ceviren-seylerdir--0906121200.html
[22] Fethullah Gülen, *Asrın Getirdiği Tereddütler 3*, Publishing İzmir 1985, p. 122.
[23] İsmail Tokalak, *Korku İmparatorluğu*, Asi Books, Istanbul 2016, p. 149.
[24] Fethullah Gülen, *Ölçü veya Yoldaki Işıklar*, Nil Publishing, İzmir 2011, p. 72.

ters" coming to terms with Gülen's thoughts on women rather than reacting to it. Let's look at Yavuz Çobanoğlu, who closely follows Gülen and his followers:

"The Gülen Movement, with the exception of the recruitment of some women simply for the purpose of showing off, never had a female actor or spokesperson. It is no secret that the inner hierarchy of the community is not suitable for women to come in to prominence. In this hierarchical structure, women can only have partial status as teachers in schools, organizations or organizers of charity bazaars, sisters of the Light Houses, but they cannot climb the ladders of hierarchy any further. For these women, male dominance is not a distraction. This acceptance is obvious. As a matter of fact, the women of the community do not care about equality at all."[25]

---

[25] Yavuz Çobanoğlu, "Asenası Eksik Bir Hareket: Gülen Cemaati", *Birikim* Journal, October 2012, No. 282, pp 83-85.

# CHAPTER V
## ADMIRATION FOR THE WEST

# ABSOLUTE AUTHORITY: THE UNITED STATES

G ülen's deep interest at the level of admiration can be easily observed in his statements. In the 80s, Gülen was pro-
claiming, *"The United States will break down. If the US has atomic
power, we have our power of faith."* He later changed his mind
in this matter like in many others. Gülen's admiration for the
West and the United Sates becomes more obvious during the
process of interfaith dialogue. Gülen praises his visit to the
United States in 1998 on his own website. Gülen accepts the
fact that the general strategy of schools established abroad has
parallels with American politics. When there happens to be
a situation of choice between Russia and the United States,
he makes clear that his choice is the United States. With this
statement Gülen answers the question of why they cannot
meet at a common ground with the AK Party's foreign policy
prioritizing "fully sovereign Turkey" and also send a message
to Latin American countries with anti-American rhetoric.
Before getting into the details of Nevval Sevindi's interview
with Gülen, let's have a look at some of his statements from
his website:

---

[1] Çoraklı, *Darbelerin Efendisi Hocia*, p. 124.

*"You cannot do business by clashing with the United States..."*

"Democracy is consolidated in the United States and other countries. Democracy's soft atmosphere includes everyone. Without establishing friendly relationship with the United States, one cannot do business anywhere in the world. If now, some voluntary organizations are establishing schools in different parts of the world with the aim of coalescing with the globe, it is impossible to implement these projects if you are in conflict with the United States. America is still the name of a nation that sits in the rudder of the world boat. The United States will play a major role in shaping the world's fate for a long time to come. This reality must be accepted. One should not try to do business here and there by ignoring the United States. You may be supported by Russia, but if you are not on good terms with the United States, you cannot do business in the world. Because the United States wants its business to go in harmony. They do not want a change in their system. The United States wants continuation of that harmony. And I do not find this odd. It should not be considered odd. The reason of our interest in the United States is that most of us raised with American and European culture anyway."[2]

It is very odd for Gülen to say that he was raised with American culture. It is a big question mark that someone who was born in a small village in Erzurum was unable to continue his education due to economic hardship, and did not even finish middle school, to claim that he was raised with American and European culture. Gülen is perhaps referring to the start of his relationship with his close friend, former CIA chief of

[2]  http://tr.fgulen.com/content/view/7877/15/

Turkey and the Middle East, Graham Fuller, taking active duty in the region in 1965. In another interview he had in New York with journalist Nevval Sevindi, although he verbally denies it, he tacitly accepts that he is in collaboration with the United States for the schools that the movement established in Turkic Republics. With this acceptance, in a way he verifies the accusations of former FBI adviser Sibel Edmonds who claimed that "the Turkish schools are an American project."[3] Let's have a look at the relevant sections in Sevindi's book, entitled, *Fetullah Gülen ile New York Sohbeti*[4]

> *"If you do not get along well with the United States, it messes up your business..."*

"The United States will play a very vital role in shaping the fate of the world for longer periods of time. This reality must be accepted. One should not try to do business here and there, disregarding the United States. If you do not get along well with the United States, then they will mess up your business. Even if the United States collapses, there will still be balances of power in the world. However, if the country with consolidated democratic philosophy, which is a major factor in the balance of the world, is shaken off, it will lead to serious chaos. The United States did not help us in the slightest bit; it does not support us solely for our own interest. If it allows us to reside here despite this fact, and if this is an advantage for us, then the United States is the one that provides us this advantage."[5]

Let's go back to the analysis by Hakan Yavuz, who produced many academic works on Fetullah Gülen and his

---

[3] *Takvim* newspaper, March 10, 2014, http://www.takvim.com.tr/Guncel/2014/03/10/cia-demek-cemaat-demek
[4] Nevval Sevindi, *Fethullah Gülen ile New York Sohbeti*, Sabah Books, Istanbul 1997.
[5] Sevindi, *Fethullah Gülen ile New York Sohbeti*, p. 6.

movement. This time let's read his interview in 2008 with Özdemir İnce about Gülen's "hesitant communication model" published in *Hürriyet* newspaper:

> *"I am concerned about the community's current state..."*

"Some communities may view me as their member. My personal opinion is that being a member of a community in Turkey has the aim of "stepping up" or "achieving certain benefits". I never needed any of those. On the other hand, I am not an anti-community person. This may seem contradictory. However, as a social scientist, I could not be disinterested in such an effective phenomenon. However, I am seriously concerned about the current "position" of the community for our democracy and for our societal peace. I voiced my concerns as an academic in Reuters as well as in many other newspapers.

> *"The community is not sincere..."*

The reasons for disturbance are: 1) The community is not sincere. It has two opposite rhetorics that are developed for domestic and international use. 2) The community has a project, and that project is not in conformity with the founding principles of the Republish of Turkey. 3) Its relations with international actors must be questioned, since its search for legitimacy both domestically and internationally made the community very vulnerable and passive. 4) The community instrumentalized Said Nursi's *Risale-i Nur* in particular and Islam in general. Day by day, an understanding of Islam without Islam became dominant. And Islamic understanding that focuses solely on power moved away from the moral core of Islam."[6]

---

[6]  Canikligil, *ABD Gizli Belgelerinde Fetullah Gülen*, pp 139-140.

Hakan Yavuz is not the only one who thinks the community is not sincere. Armenian Argentinean Pablo Kendikian, who is preparing a book on Fetullah Gülen and his movement, also thinks that Gülen "uses religion as a cover for his political interests". He draws attention to Gülen's contrasting rhetoric in his interview published in *Diario Armenia*:

> *"Even if the Gülen Movement is a religious community, its real aim is political..."*

> "I think that the Argentinean Foreign Ministry should re-evaluate the movement's stance as a religious establishment through registered religions because, although the Gülen Movement is openly a religious community, their aims are political. The movement introduced itself strategically as the defendant of interfaith dialogue that is distanced from politics. However, this rhetoric is in opposition with its intensive involvement in the Turkish political structure."

> "The Gülen Movement is a project of power and in each region it operates, it employs different political strategies. One of their peculiar characteristics is their long-term planning. The power that mobilizes the movement was the utopia to develop neo-Ottomanism within and without the Ottoman Empire. I can state that this idea is globa. It is a modern version of Pan-Turcism".[7]

## The reason behind not returning Turkey: "The fear of losing his gains"

We remember how Gülen, to whose contradictory statements we come across very often, answered in tears the calls

---

[7] http://www.diarioarmenia.org.ar/el-movimiento-gulen-al-descubierto-trama-y-objetivos/

to him by Prime Minister Erdoğan to "come back to the country".[8] Gülen linked his reason for not returning to the country to his concerns that "the country may be harmed". We do not know whether or not the reason for Gülen not returning to the country he missed so much was his fear of the mysterious web of relations he had established in the US since 1998 being revealed. Let's listen to Gülen's concerns on this matter from him own mouth:

> "Now let me say he [Erdoğan] did what suited him. However, I should say that he is not the first one to behave this way. Both the president and prime minister sent me their invitations either publicly or through messengers. Other state elites, too, did do their best at all times in this matter. I have heard this many times. They ask, isn't it time to return to Turkey? They do what suits them. I think – in this matter, it is not suitable to say I, but – I should do what suits me. Now, they invite me and say 'come back!' That is normal... The public may also think the same. If they do not call, I could not go to Turkey anyway. Turkey is not a stable and secure place. For this reason I may get myself into trouble. The things I present may be such inappropriate things. I never lived with the fear of getting into trouble...."[9]

It is not clear what Gülen means by these vague statements. It is obvious that his confusion reflects on his language. Let's read another passage in which he more explicitly expresses his concerns:

*"If the gains will be lost, then I would not want to go back..."*

"If we have a wish, if we have a dream, that is Turkey not having new problems, that the country would not expe-

[8]   https://www.youtube.com/watch?v=lqLt6XxByJs
[9]   https://www.youtube.com/watch?v=lqLt6XxByJs

rience new distress. If there is only 1 percent chance of losing some of our gains, with this concern, not for myself though, with that concern, I would not want to go back. If I see any prospect that would eradicate my concerns, then I, this poor servant, would think about that. Of course, saying that "I would think" is a form of ego-centric thought. That's why I should not say that. If I sense that some people who hold grudges against me in Turkey would harm some institutions and put the government in a difficult position (even if it was a 1 percent chance); and some other people would stop the positive developments in Turkey after I return to Turkey, then I would stay here for a longer period, in order not to harm the good things in my country. I would live here with the dream of going back to Turkey. I would live with the memory of the coffees that I drank in Turkey. Then I would escape from these feelings when they encroached upon me. And continue living like this here perhaps forever."[10]

## Confusing Affinity: Graham Fuller's admiration for Gülen...

It is a very clear fact that the support of a former CIA Chief of Turkey and the Middle East, Graham Fuller, played a critical role in turning Gülen and his community into a global movement. Neither Fuller, nor Gülen denounced their relationship so far. We will present the articles of Fuller in support of Gülen after the failed July 15 coup attempt in the following sections. However, let's have a look at another important detail that Fuller stated on Gülen. In 2004, in the book he wrote his experiences on the Middle East titled *The Future of Political Islam* (*Siyasal İslam'ın Geleceği*), he tells about the distance

---

[10] Canikligil, *ABD Gizli Belgelerinde Fetullah Gülen*, pp 158-159.

between the army and seculars as he calls *"Turkey's radical seculars"* and Gülen as follows:

> *"The seculars and the army worry that Gülen will capture the government..."*

"This movement, attributing to the most influential and broad segment is still led by the Gülen Movement. Classical sharia does not play a central role in the thinking of the movement. The movement does not have a literal understanding of Islamic text but makes interpretations in the light of today's developments. In this regard, the outlook of the movement is very modernist. The Gülen Movement is rationalist and gives great importance to tolerance in a pluralist community. It is a known fact that, in the schools that Fetullah supporters had established in Turkey and abroad, there is quality and secular education both in English and in Turkish.

Although Fetullah supporters do not have the aim of establishing a political party, the leader of the party gives unbounding advice to the followers, numbering in the millions, on whom to vote in the elections. Most of the members were represented slightly in traditional Turkish parties and even in Islamist parties. Seculars think that although the Nur movement is apolitical in character, in the long term they have destructive and even dangerous aims to place religious activists into the state apparatus."[11]

For sure, Fuller is not making these analyses because he perceives Gülen and his community as a threat. He tries to create an image of a "modern religious person" who does not deserve these accusations. He presents Gülen as a tolerant

[11] Graham E. Fuller, *The Future of Political Islam*, Palgrave Macmillan, US 2003, pp 220-223.

Muslim. In a way, so as not to give leverage to anti-Gülen circles in the United States, he deliberately brings the accusations into the picture as a tactic of precaution. It is obvious that, Fuller, writing articles supporting Gülen, does not think that the allegations he made years ago can be right. Or this way serves his purpose well. Let's have a look at his article in *The Huffington Post* in which he feverishly opposes the claims that the Gülen Movement is a "cult":

> *"The Gülen Movement is a rational, moderate, positive and open minded movement..."*

"I do not believe that the last week's unsuccessful coup attempt against Erdoğan was organized by Gülen. Naturally, it is not possible to say anything precise without evidence. Erdoğan already struck a blow on the community before the coup. Erdoğan got mad because of the news of corruption that were revealed by Gülen supporters in 2013. He started to attack members, supporters, workers, TV channels, newspapers, schools and social institutions of the Hizmet movement. The movement was smitten. For this reason, to prevent Erdoğan's rising power and continuation of democracy, its members establish relations with liberal and secular forces for the purpose of returning to a military order.

> *"Gülen supported the 1980 coup to protect the state from harm"*

Gülen emphasized the importance of the state's honor and dignity. He always canonized the state against Islamic movements' understanding of putting Islam before the state. He went to the extent of supporting the 1980 coup to protect the state from harm. On the other hand, Gülen defends that for the Hizmet movement to thrive freely, and continue its social mission, democracy is needed, not a military government. The movement never engaged in any terrorist activities. For this reason, its support even for political violence is out of question. Erdoğan's conceptualization of the movement as a 'terrorist structure' will be absurd for those who have even the slightest knowledge on the movement, because it gives great importance to peace and dialogue.

### *"I was a guarantor for Gülen..."*

I wrote the reference letter for Gülen's application for a Green Card to the United States in 2008. I indicated that I do not believe that Gülen may be a security threat to the United States. My approval for the Green Card, coincides with the timeframe when I had finished my book titled *The Future of Political Islam*. While preparing this book, I had examined the Hizmet movement as a moderate, tolerant, non-aggressive, social movement open to dialogue rather than a political movement that would give utmost importance to education. However, within the Bush administration's global war on terror policy, Gülen wanted to be deported. As a CIA official, I asked the FBI to take my judgements on Gülen into consideration.

### *"In the future, Islam will be represented by the Gülen Movement..."*

Well, which movements will represent Islam in the future? Is it ISIS? Is it al-Qaida? Is it the Muslim Brotherhood? I would put the Hizmet movement on top of the list as it is a rational, moderate, positive, open minded movement. Hizmet is not a cult. It is a movement in the center for the modernization of Islam. Erdoğan's AKP was like that once upon a time. However, over time, Erdoğan became greedy for power. For the last couple of years, he is destroying everything that his party had accumulated. Well, what will be the end of it? Erdoğan vanquished Hizmet. On the other hand, he is sowing the seeds of his own destruction. Turkey is becoming a "pariah" in the international arena."[12]

Fuller states that after September 11, Gülen had some problems with state officials. Thanks to Fuller's support, Gülen was able to secure a residency permit. Thus, conforming our information on giving Gülen a reference letter, he also enabled us to obtain to new detail. However there are some contradictory statements in his writings. For some reason, Fuller is quite persistent that there is no way for Gülen to have any links to the July 15 coup while he states that Gülen supported the 1980 military coup "to protect the state from harm". Fuller, as we will examine in the coming section, praises someone who originally instrumentalized democracy and freedom, but after the coup attempt, he supported democracy and freedom. If we take the United States wars to "bring democracy and freedom" into consideration, then it would be "normal" for Fuller to support military operations on the way to democracy. It is not a distant memory, how the Western world and the American administration blessed and legitimized the coup plotters after the recent bloody coup in Egypt. Let's not deviate from the main topic and go back to Fuller's statement on Gülen. Fuller, has detailed analysis of Gülen and his community in his latest book titled *Turkey and Arab Spring in 2014.* It is not hard to understand the mission that Fuller ascribes to Gülen. He explicitly states that he would like to put Gülen and his community at the center as a representative Islamic movement. For this reason, Fuller does not like the

[12] http://www.huffingtonpost.com/graham-e-fuller/gulen-movement-not-cult_b_11116858.html

possibility of interruption of aforesaid projects due to rising anti- Gülen sentiments after December 17/25, 2013 and July 15, 2016 in Turkey. Let's continue to read Fuller's analysis of the "community" to understand the special mission that Fuller gives to Gülen:

*"The Gülen Movement is the world's most powerful, efficient and biggest Islamic movement...."*

"In the present situation of international violence, war, unfairness, fanaticism, and the Middle East's transient problems; Islam's traditional norms like civic responsibility, tolerance, social justice and moderation are being interrupted. This is a source of key concern for many Muslims. This kind of poisonous environment, increasing insecurity, desperation, intolerance, contributes to radicalism. It is these dangerous tendencies that the Turkey-based Fetullah Gülen faith movement is fighting against today. The Gülen Movement is the world's broadest and the most powerful Islamic movement that prioritizes moderation, tolerance and is in search for modernity in Islam.

The Gülen Movement is the most powerful example of popular Islam. From time to time, it is called the community (jamaat) in Turkey but the movement calls itself "Hizmet". Presently, Hizmet is the most efficient, and most populous movement in Turkey. As an idiosyncratic grassroots organization with the combination of unusual qualifications like the modernization of faith through social voluntary work for humanity; the adoption of science and religion as complementary concepts; its program for the extension of education; its call for ethnic and religious tolerance; its claim that it does not clash with the West; and its interfaith dialogue efforts; it started to gain prominence in most parts of the Muslim world as well as beyond it. Gülen works to curb radical tendencies, and to return to the embedded values of Islam like social responsibilities, social justice, and rational analysis. Not surprisingly, Hizmet's growing efficiency and wealth created frustration among the secularists who are against religion to gain strength in public life, due to concerns for Hizmet's effect on the government and its long term-plans. The latest clash with the AKP has positive effect for Hizmet's public profile.

...Gülen was also inspired by many Turkish modern Muslim intellectuals and poet, Jalaluddin Rumi. However, Gülen chose to transfer this inspiration to more practical, social and organizational forms rather than to an ascetic form. The movement began to make an impact beyond Turkey's borders... At a time when the Muslim world turned to ruin because of chaos, radical theologies, and violence in the name of Islamic salvation, Hizmet is the manifestation of modern and moderate values of Islam and an element of popular balance....

Fetullah Gülen, who is an emotional preacher and mentor, has a powerful fan base. Ironically enough, he is an introverted person. In both of the opportunities I had to interview with him, I was struck with old-fashioned shyness, unpretentiousness and kindness. His Turkish is full of symbolic expressions and Ottoman-Turkish idioms. His interpretations of current events are inclined to be cautious, and he prefers to talk about those issues in a disguised form. He is proficient in Arabic and Farsi, and tried to learn English; he seems to be knowledgeable on current world matters. Everyone who respects him, refers to him as *Hoca Efendi, meaning 'the esteemed hodja".*[13]

[13] Graham E. Fuller, *Türkiye ve Arap Baharı*, int.. Mustafa Acar, Eksi Kitaplar, Ankara 2014, pp 203-210.

Fuller, does not hide his admiration while he gives detailed information on Gülen's mission. Let's move on to the sections where Fuller interprets Gülen's philosophy:

*"According to Gülen the very heart of the matter is first being human, then being Muslim..."*

"Throughout time, Gülen extended his area of interest to include the appreciation of shared human values. These values should not come solely from Islam; he thinks that similar values are present in other religions, especially in Judaism and Christianity. As if, Islamic values are stripped from traditional Islamic rituals, theology and culture and put into a new framework. These values are not linked to peculiar cultural Muslim means. It can even be called "Non-Muslim Islam" – Islamic values that reach beyond a peculiar Muslim culture – to reach a common goal on education, social service, interfaith dialogue and general welfare to reach a common goal. Substantially, Gülen mentions "First being human then being Muslim". Hence, Gülen's vision does not only defend personal philosophical development but at the same time, it defends social activism, including voluntarism that will enable the construction of a new society. As Gülen said, *'This new people will combine a deep spirituality, extensive knowledge, concrete thoughts, scientific nature, and aphorism with activism. They will never be satisfied with what they know alone, they will always increase their knowledge on the self, nature and Allah.'*[14] Fundamentally, what makes hundreds of thousands of Turks and others to internalize this mission, to establish schools abroad, to provide social services inside Turkey and abroad, is this voluntarism and personal devotion.

[14] http://fgulen.org/about-fethullah-gulen/gulens-thoughts/1294-the-new-man-and-woman.html

This situation is very different from the suspicious Muslims who look askance at the West. Gülen's ideas of prosperity and modernity do not aim to imitate Western life style but construction of a freed Muslim mind that will function confidently in the modern world."[15]

It is needless to state once again how strategic and deep is the mission that Fuller ascribes to Gülen. Fuller already states the matter in its most minute details. However, Fuller's exclusion of all the other Islamic factions as *"Suspicious Muslims who look at the West with suspicion"* definitely shows in his analysis. Fuller, in his analysis of Gülen's Islamic model, does not mention the deep drifts in the past. Gülen's statements on his secret mission that he shares with his followers in private talks and sermons, apparently does not mean anything for Fuller. In this situation, it is possible to make two deductions: The first one is that Fuller really believes that Gülen had evolved in to a controllable, obedient, harmless individual compatible with the "Islamization Project."[16] And as the director of the project, he has a calm attitude. The second one is that he knows that radical rhetoric is necessary to collect supporters at some periods of time. Both deductions mean that the plan is under control so that Fuller's calm attitude has meaning despite the rising anti-Gülenism in the West.

## Fuller's analysis is subjective

Fuller continues to share his opinions in his book. However, as the book is written in 2004, at a time when the Gülen-AK

---

[15] Fuller, *Türkiye ve Arap Bahanı*, p. 208.
[16] Islamization Project/Green Belt: A Protestant and modernist interpretation of Islam having intelligence links that was developed by the West to prevent political instability that can harm their interest caused by increased radical Islamist activities in Islamic countries during the Cold War.

Party struggle was new, it causes some of Fuller's subjective analysis to collapse. Fuller, trying to cover up the contradictions of Gülen and his community, does not feel the need to comparatively analyze the Gülenist media's statements during and after the Ergenekon process. For example, while they were saying, "one cannot be considered a journalist if they wear journalism as a shield",[17] during the Ergenekon process, after the 2013 events they were saying, "every attempt to curb the freedom of media is against democracy and cannot be accepted".[18] On the contrary, he interprets the declaration of Journalists and Writers Foundation of April 2013 as a "blow to Erdoğan".[19] Let us continue to present Fuller's analysis:

> "Gülen, joined the liberals and opposition parties on criticizing the AKP publicly about the debated issue of Erdoğan's attempt to drown criticism. Gülen's flag ship Journalists and Writers Foundation, issued harsh declaration on the freedom of media on April 2013. This is an open blow to Erdoğan. Referring to EU norms and mentioning the long time illnesses of the Turkish media, the declaration reads: 'For example, any attempt that limits freedom of press like political pressure, business interest and self-censor is against democracy and is unacceptable'. Journalists were invited to protect 'the honor and principles of journalism' and 'putting media under pressure' by media bosses for protecting the interest of politicians or the protection of their business interest are condemned straightforwardly...

> ...Erdoğan, started to be more and more concerned about the impact of the Gülen Movement, as a potential ri-

---

[17] Ekrem Dumanlı, *Zaman* Newspaper, March 7, 2011.
[18] Journalist and Writers Foundation, April 2013, Press Conference.
[19] Fuller, *Türkiye ve Arap Baharı*, p. 234.

val power, among pious Turks; especially because of the probability of Gülen supporters' encouragement to withdraw support from the AKP in the coming elections...

*"Hizmet's power comes from its followers' wealth and devotion..."*

...Some analysts mentioned Hizmet may establish a political party by extending its strong organization to the realm of politics. In principle, there is no obstacle for Hizmet to establish a political party. However, this step is not very likely to be taken, because this will injure the declared values and appeal. The functions of a movement are quite different from those of a political party. Politics is the art of things that are possible. Politics requires to set aside many ideals to function in the realities of daily politics that can create enemies easily. The open split between the AKP and Gülen in 2013, if Hizmet wanted, presented a great opportunity for establishing a religious political party as an alternative to the AK Party, however Hizmet did not do it. Engaging in formal political activity may risk Hizmet's reputation of social and educational activities... The power of Hizmet comes from the wealth, devotion and activism of its supporters, not from the political distribution of power. This situation does not mean that Gülen will not speak on the key national matters that he thinks a regulatory intervention is needed."[20]

*"Erdoğan will probably be the biggest loser..."*

Some tendencies will be successful while others will not. In the ugly inclemency between Erdoğan and Hizmet, Erdoğan will probably be the biggest loser. Many non-Gülenist supporters also condemn Erdoğan's attitude and do not accredit his attacks on Gülen. Meanwhile, Gülen is

---

[20] Fuller, *Türkiye ve Arap Baharı*, pp 235-236.

in a solid and principled position on criticizing corruption in higher echelons."[21]

Graham Fuller, in an interview with BBC Turkish in 2014, answers claims on "Gülen establishing a state within the state" as follows:

"The biggest criticism to Hizmet can be that, it is not transparent. For decades, they were seen as a destructive and dangerous movement, and they were oppressed. I believe these statements do not describe the movement correctly. However, Hizmet's psychology is changing. For years, they thought that they were attacked by the Kemalist state. They could not get into the military, they were denied from important offices in Turkish bureaucracy. They were seen as "obscurantists". This view is now changing. I do not think that the so-called "clash" between the AKP and Hizmet is as serious and as deep as it has been asserted. Now, it is an individual problem based on characters. I believe that in general they share the same vision. The future of this "clash" depends on Erdoğan's personality and his uneasiness and insecurity on his own position in the government. When it comes to the word "infiltrate", yes I also think that it has a negative connotation. However, also in the United States, when the Democrats or Republicans come to power, they aim to fill the bureaucratic offices with their supporters. We do not call it infiltration. However, if Hizmet uses government institutions for its own interest, then there is something to worry about."[22]

It is not clear whether the reasons Fuller states for Gülen's not establishing a political party are analyses or advice. How-

---

[21] Fuller, *Türkiye ve Arap Baharı*, p. 240.

[22] http://www.bbc.com/turkce/haberler/2014/06/140620_graham_fuller_roportaj

ever, one thing is very clear that, Hizmet, what he called a political rival to the AK Party, despite Gülen's intense opposition and criticism, had a major defeat in 2014 both in local[23] and presidential[24] elections. Fuller's claim that Erdoğan will be the biggest loser in the long run, is a deviation in analysis and a big misfortune that a respectful academic would never want to experience.

## According to FBI Adviser Edmonds, "Gülen is a symbol for CIA..."

Another name that had followed Gülen closely for many years is Sibel Edmonds, who worked for the FBI as a translator and adviser and currently works as a journalist. Contrary to Fuller, Edmonds takes a more suspicious approach to Gülen and his community. Edmonds states that the CIA uses Gülen to weaken President Erdoğan and Gülen is just a symbol, nothing more for the CIA. What Edmonds said in 2014 is very important:

> *"CIA brought Gülen to USA..."*

> "I lived in Turkey for a very long time and I closely follow Turkish politics. Americans are surprised, and they ask, "How did Erdoğan, once an angel, become a demon, an enemy for the US?" Erdoğan's befall started with his clash with Fetullah Gülen. Gülen is just a symbol. The more important is his trade mark. After 1997, the CIA included Gülen in the game. The CIA brought him to the states and what a coincidence that placed him in a house just beside

---

[23] The AK Party was the the winner of March 30, 2014 elections and got 42.87% of votes.

[24] In the first presidential elections held on August 10, 2014. Recep Tayyip Erdoğan, received 51.79% of votes and was elected president in the first round.

CIA headquarters. Gülen has been living in the States for 15 years and he is controlling a web worth 20-25 billion dollars. Moreover, nobody knows the source of this money. The Gülen Movement and the CIA established a big media network and they infiltrated the police force and military by buying out people.

*"Their biggest supporter is Jewish lobbies..."*

"When Erdoğan got powerful, he defied this structure. This defiance was also against to the CIA and all other deep structures that are behind the 'Gülen' trade mark. Another reason was Erdoğan's firm stance against Israel and that he appeared to have a say in relations with Israel. Despite the media and all political parties, it was Fetullah Gülen who criticized this situation. Gülen's biggest supporters in the United States are the Jewish lobbies. At this point, another event broke out; the Gezi Park incidents. Gülen wanted to put this incident to good use in his clash with Erdoğan. Gülen, thus, incorporated people from his community to these protests. Erdoğan understood what will happen to him. The CIA stepped in and started to play an active role in the protests. At the same time, both in European and American media Erdoğan started to be mentioned as a 'dictator'. It is a known fact that the CIA establishes puppet governments and destroys them overnight. The same thing is being done to Erdoğan. On the other hand, Gülen schools established outside of Turkey with the help of the CIA, were closing down, because these countries had realized that the Gülen Movement's presence is a threat to their national security as it was used by the CIA in joint operations."[25]

---

[25] http://www.takvim.com.tr/guncel/2014/03/10/cia-demek-cemaat-demek

Let's continue to read Edmonds' statement that Jewish lobbies are Gülen's biggest supporters and how she describe these set of events as an operation against President Erdoğan:

*"Jewish support for Gülen is a question mark..."*

"What is interesting is that, Gülen, an Islamist imam, is supported by the Jewish lobby. The Jewish lobby would never support an Islamic model. Even this reason alone would be enough for people to feel suspicious about Gülen and start to ask questions. This was the second reason for the clash between Erdoğan and Gülen. That is to say, Gülen's being supported by the Jewish lobbies, does not approve Erdoğan's firm stance against Israel. It was time for separation. And then follows the Syria issue. There was the allegation that 'Turkey, the AK Party government arms and trains the opposition forces in Syria and all these are directed by the US from İncirlik Air Base. Up until this point, everything was fine. Erdoğan and the American administration were on good terms. They were doing everything to overthrow the Assad regime. However, something unexpected happened. The deep structure in the US which is against Obama, convinced people that Assad was under pressure. The States' interference was not approved. Obama was losing support on this matter. At this point, Russia entering the picture, forced the United State to take a step back. Right at this point, the Turkish public opinion was injected with the idea that "Relations with Assad had gone sour because of the opposition".

*"CIA and Gülen played an active role in the Gezi Park incidents..."*

"When the States stepped back, Erdoğan was left alone. From that moment on, he was a hated leader, rather than loved among his people. The States was not keeping any of its promises and was leaving him alone, and that annoyed Erdoğan very much. This happens to be the third reason. At this point another incident broke out: the Gezi Park protests. Gülen wanted to take advantage of this incident in his clash with Erdoğan, and encouraged his followers to support the protests. Erdoğan understood what will happen to him. The CIA and Gülen stepped in and played an active role in the protests. Erdoğan was very much aware of what was really happening."[26]

Sibel Edmonds claims that the disagreement began with Syria policies and deepened with the Gezi Park events. In both of these incidents, the president underwent a CIA-backed perception operation. What Edmonds says is important for various reasons. It can be clearly seen one more times that, the Gezi Park events, that consolidated all opposition to Erdoğan under one roof, was not solely a democratic reflex of opposition groups. Here we need to note one very important point. After the investigations, it has been proven that public officials who enabled the Gezi Park events to reach the extent of a coup attempt, burned down the tents, and used disproportionate force, were indeed members of the 'parallel gang' who were gathered together in the state as bureaucratic oligarchs."[27] This fact supports Edmonds' analysis. Let's continue to read Edmonds' analysis:

*"The problems between Erdoğan and Gülen harm the CIA's goals..."*

"Erdoğan and the AK Party are just symbols; like puppet governments in the other countries; like Obama; and like

---

[26] https://www.youtube.com/watch?v=gRx8S5YTdJk&feature=youtu.be&app=desktop

[27] http://www.star.com.tr/acikgorus/turkiyenin-burokratik-oligark-ile-imtihani-haber-1121023/

George Bush. The most important thing to understand is the real power that controls these symbols; namely, the CIA, and the American weapon industry. The CIA's goal was to control the country in question and govern its international and domestic politics in full... The CIA's plan was to use Turkey as a model and align all other countries, and put the moderate Islam project into practice in the Middle East. The problems between Erdoğan and Gülen (read CIA) were hindering these plans... Erdoğan, to amplify the problems with the CIA, staked it all. To show that he will not bow down, to give a message, Erdoğan said, "I will buy billions of dollars worth of weapons from China but not from the US". The whole world was shocked with his stake. This meant breaking one of the top rules of the US and NATO. This could be the last thing to do. This infuriated NATO and the American weapon industry."[28]

*"Erdoğan violated Western codes..."*

"And Erdoğan went even further and said, 'They had waited for years to be a member of the EU. Now, he understood that it is not going to happen. Instead of the EU, they want to be a member of Sanghai Five", and he officially applied for it. This behavior, was once again another code violation. Turkey, which has been a puppet of the West for a century, now rebelled against its puppet master. The west will not let this puppet system to be easily destroyed. When you do things like that, it means you had reached your expiration date. It is over no matter who you are. And the punishment that the US will give should be exemplary because this situation could be imitated by others, and this risk may not be taken."[29]

---

[28] https://www.youtube.com/watch?v=gRx8S5YTdJk&feature=youtu.be&app=desktop
[29] http://www.timeturk.com/tr/2014/02/27/cia-erdogan-i-neden-hedef-aldi.html

## RAND's "Civil Democratic Islam" Report

One of the most prominent think tanks of the United States, RAND, published a report in 2003 by Cheryl Benard titled, *"Civil Democratic Islam: Partners, Sources and Strategies"*.[30] The report analyzes recent developments in the Islamic world in detail. Graham Fuller also works for RAND. A well-known "think tank", RAND closely analyzes the Islamic world and prepares thematic reports for the CIA. However, what's interesting is that, in the United States' text listing the objectives aimed at the Islamic world, Fetullah Gülen and his community being presented to the public is included in the moderate Islam section as a method of fighting radical Islam in the long term. Let's have a look at an abstract of the report in which Cheryl Benard states "Fetullah Gülen was mainly effected by Sufism. Nevertheless, Fetullah Gülen put forward a modern version of Islam. Tolerance, variety and non-violence are emphasized in this version of Islam". RAND's report becomes more meaningful after Sibel Edmonds' analysis.

> *"Moderate Islamists will be helped to establish schools and institutions..."*

"Support the modernists first: Publish and distribute their works at subsidized cost; encourage them to write for mass audiences and for youth; introduce their views into the curriculum of Islamic education. Give them a public platform; make their opinions and judgments on fundamental questions of religious interpretation available to a mass audience in competition with those of the fundamentalists and traditionalists, who have websites,

---

[30] Cheryl Benard, *Civil Democratic Islam: Partners, Resources and Strategies*, RAND Corporation, 2003.

publishing houses, schools, institutes, and many other vehicles for disseminating their views; position secularism and modernism as a "counterculture" option for disaffected Islamic youth; facilitate and encourage an awareness of their pre- and non-Islamic history and culture, in the media and the curricula of relevant countries; and assist in the development of independent civic organizations, to promote civic culture and provide a space for ordinary citizens to educate themselves about the political process and to articulate their views.

Support the traditionalists against the fundamentalists: Publicize traditionalist criticism of fundamentalist violence and extremism; encourage disagreements between traditionalists and fundamentalists; discourage alliances between traditionalists and fundamentalists. Encourage cooperation between modernists and the traditionalists who are closer to the modernist end of the spectrum. Encourage the popularity and acceptance of Sufism. Confront and oppose the fundamentalists: Challenge their interpretation of Islam and expose inaccuracies. Reveal their linkages to illegal groups and activities. Publicize the consequences of their violent acts. Encourage journalists to investigate issues of corruption, hypocrisy, and immorality in fundamentalist and terrorist circles. Encourage divisions among fundamentalists.

Selectively support secularists: Encourage recognition of fundamentalism as a shared enemy, discourage secularist alliance with anti-U.S. Forces on such grounds as nationalism and leftist ideology."[31]

---

[31] Cheryl Benard, *Civil Democratic Islam: Partners, Resources and Strategies*, RAND, 2003, ix-xii http://www.rand.org/content/dam/rand/pubs/monograph_reports/2005/MR1716.pdf

The report holds very important details. In the section titled *"Strategy in Depth"* the road map and actions to be taken to spread modernist Islam are discussed in detail. Let's continue to read the section titled *"Basic points of Strategy"*:

"Clearly, the United States, the modern industrialized world, and indeed the international community as a whole would prefer an Islamic world that is compatible with the rest of the system: democratic, economically viable, politically stable, socially progressive, and follows the rules and norms of international conduct. They also want to prevent a "clash of civilizations" in all of its possible variants—from increased domestic unrest caused by conflicts between Muslim minorities and "native" populations in the West to increased militancy across the Muslim world and its consequences, instability and terrorism.

Islam's current crisis has two main components: a failure to thrive and a loss of connection to the global mainstream. The Islamic world has been marked by a long period of backwardness and comparative powerlessness; many different solutions, such as nationalism, pan-Arabism, Arab socialism, and Islamic revolution, have been attempted without success, and this has led to frustration and anger. At the same time, the Islamic world has fallen out of step with contemporary global culture, an uncomfortable situation for both sides. Following an eclectic approach combining the following components may yield to an effective outcome:

*First, the reformers must be supported, by:*

Enhancing their vision of Islam over that of the traditionalists by providing them with a broad platform to articulate and disseminate their views - publishing and distribute their works — encouraging them to write for mass audiences and youth — introducing their views into the curriculum of Islamic education — giving them a public platform — making their opinions and judgments on fundamental questions of religious interpretation available to a mass audience, in competition with those of the fundamentalists and traditionalists, who already have Web sites, publishing houses, schools, institutes, and many other vehicles for disseminating their views — positioning modernism as a "counterculture" option for disaffected Islamic youth — facilitating and encouraging awareness of pre- and non-Islamic history and culture, in the media and in the curricula of relevant countries — encouraging and supporting secular civic and cultural institutions and programs.

*Supporting traditionalists against fundamentalists, by:*

Publicizing traditionalist criticism of fundamentalist violence and extremism and encouraging disagreements between traditionalists and fundamentalists — preventing alliances between traditionalists and fundamentalists — encouraging cooperation between modernists and traditionalists who are closer to that end of the spectrum, increase the presence and profile of modernists in traditionalist institutions — discriminating between different sectors of traditionalism — encouraging those with a greater affinity to modernism—such as the Hanafi law school as opposed to others to issue religious opinions that, by becoming popularized, can weaken the authority of backward Wahhabi religious rulings — encouraging the popularity and acceptance of Sufism.

*Confront and oppose the fundamentalists, by:*

Challenging and exposing the inaccuracies in their views

on questions of Islamic interpretation — exposing their relationships with illegal groups and activities — publicizing the consequences of their violent acts — demonstrating their inability to rule to the benefit and positive development of their communities — targeting these messages especially to young people, to pious traditionalist populations, to Muslim minorities in the West, and to women — avoiding showing respect or admiration for the violent feats of fundamentalist extremists and terrorists, instead casting them as disturbed and cowardly rather than evil heroes — encouraging journalists to investigate issues of corruption, hypocrisy, and immorality in fundamentalist and terrorist circles

*Selectively support secularists, by:*

— encouraging recognition of fundamentalism as a shared enemy, discouraging secularist alliances with anti-U.S. forces on such grounds as nationalism and leftist ideology — supporting the idea that religion and the state can be separate in Islam, too, and that this does not endanger the faith."[32]

[32] Cheryl Benard, *Civil Democratic Islam: Partners, Resources and Strategies*, pp 61-65.

CHAPTER VI
**REPORT CARD ON DEMOCRACY**

# DEMOCRACY AND FREEDOM

In Gülen's philosophy, "democracy" and "freedom" are treated as if they are vitally important concepts, but in reality, they are used as instrumental and conjuncture-bound terms. For Gülen, all kinds of means are justified to reach yje "Supreme Goal". For that reason, in his messages for the West, he acts like a democratic, and modern "scholar", while in the community's domestic politics and hierarchy, he is an oppressive and authoritarian "leader". Before getting into Gülen's paradoxical approaches and statements on democracy and freedom, let's read American journalist Claire Berlinski's article titled, "Who is Fetullah Gulen?" published in *City Journal* in 2012, where she draws our attention to the "oppressive understanding within the community":

> *"The internal structure of the community is anti-democratic and oppressive..."*

"The movement's supporters say that its structure is informal — that being "inspired" by Gülen is akin to being "inspired" by Mother Teresa. Critics, including many people who have left the movement, observe that its organizational structure is strict, hierarchical, and undemocratic. Gülen (known to his followers as *Hocaefendi*, or "master teacher") is the sole leader, they say, and each community is led by *abis*, or elder brothers, who are privy to only a limited amount of information. Sociologist Berna Turam has argued that the *abis* make strong suggestions about, and perhaps dictate, whom members should marry. Even if prospective spouses are not within the *cemaat*, the *cemaat* should benefit from them; a spouse from a rich or powerful family would be an asset, for example.... . Ilhan Tanır, a Turkish journalist who was in the *cemaat* but who left it, has expressed particular concern about the blind obedience demanded of its members. Moreover, Tanır holds, the *cemaat* believes that its cosmic mission "justifies any conduct to achieve its ends at any cost."[1]

It is not surprising for those who are familiar with the community's working methods to read news on İlhan Tanır[2] who had left the community and levelled important criticism to Gülen in 2012, that says Tanır was one of the closest names to Gülen. Tanır's transformation shows that Gülen's "ambivalent politics model" is the "dominant ideology" that effected each and every follower from top to bottom.

Let's have a look at the facility manager of the Golden Generation Worship and Recreation Center, Bekir Aksoy's interview with Suzan Hansen in Pennsylvania in 2010, that was published in *The New Republic*. Hansen relates one anecdote told by Bekir Aksoy as an example for Gülen supporters' absolute obedience:

> "At the end of my tour, as Aksoy was driving me back to a McDonald's near the Camp where I had left my car, I asked him whether Gülen tells people what to do. "He would

[1] Claire Berlinski, "Who is Fethullah Gulen?", *City Journal*, 2012.
[2] http://www.medyagundem.com/fetonun-abddeki-tetikcisinin-son-skandali/

never tell; he *suggests*," Aksoy replied. "And then what do people do with that suggestion?" I asked. "Let me put it this way," he said. "If a man with a Ph.D. and a career came to see Hocaefendi, and Hocaefendi told him it might be a good idea to build a village on the North Pole, that man with a Ph.D. would be back the next morning with a suitcase."[3]

## The problem of Multiculturalism

What Gülen wrote many years ago in one of his books on "the culture of living together" is a very telling example on the drifts of his mind.

*" A Muslim believer who accepts to be under the rule of an infidel does not have the right to live..."*

"The Islamic way of life needs to dominate life in general. It is incumbent upon us to represent this trust in our activities. A Muslim believer should live with this ideal throughout his life and for this ideal, they should set sail to cold and hot seas... From the glaciers of Siberia to North and South America, wherever they go, they make their power and dominance felt. Because Allah would not accept a Muslim living under the dominance of an infidel. If this Muslim believer had agreed to live under the tutelage of an infidel, then it means he lost everything that belongs to Islam and faith. A person like this does not deserve to live. His life would be miserable....And his next world be miserable as well. For this reason, the holiest idea that a Muslim believer should keep alive with rigor should be the desire for world domination."[4]

---

[3]  https://newrepublic.com/article/79062/global-turkey-imam-fethullah-gulen
[4]  Fethullah Gülen, *İlâ-yı Kelimetullah veya Cihad*, Nil Publishing, İzmir 2001, p. 148

## 1971 Memorandum

To understand Gülen's intellectual background and codes, one needs to look closer at his attitudes, behaviors and statements in transitional periods. We know that, after the 1971 memorandum, Gülen was arrested and put into prison. Gülen, on different occasions, tells stories about his prison days and his distress after the memorandum.[5] His analysis about the memorandum that harmed the community's planning, is very interesting. Before getting into this, let's read evaluations of Bediüzzaman Said Nursi's former lawyer Bekir Berk on the period. Bekir Berk is an important name because of the fame he acquired due to his close relationship with Bediüzzaman Said Nursi and his efficiency and prestige among the *Nurcus*. Besides, he is a lawyer who defended the arrested *Nurcus after the 1971 memorandum*. The 1971 memorandum, a disgrace in Turkish political history, is depicted by Bekir Berk on February 10, 1971 in *Yeni Asya* newspaper as follows:

> "This voice is the voice of our history. This voice is like a voice coming from Mohaç. This voice raises from Malazgirt. This voice echoes veterans of Kanije. This voice is the voice of our soldiers, this voice is the voice of protectors of our freedom and independence, this voice is the voice of our honorable pashas, of our honor, religion and faith... This voice is not the voice of people who punch the air aimlessly, this is the voice of those who would know and see where the danger is coming from, this is the voice of those who fight against that danger, and give the order to "get ready," for the very last time."[6]

---

[5]    Aytekin Gezici, *Okyanus Ötesi Gerçeği*, Anatolia Books, Istanbul 2011, pp 58-63.
[6]    Bekir Berk, *Çağ ve Nesil* Journal, No. 9, May 1984.

Berk's statements summarize the "Nur movement's" attitude towards the military. Although Gülen does not accept it,[7] he was a member of that movement, and his analysis is not different from Berk's. He depicts his satisfaction with military intervention as follows:

*"The 1971 Memorandum is bad. In comparison, however, it is not as bad as the worse..."*

"The memorandum was formally given after the reading of the statement on radio on Friday, March 12 at 1:00 p.m. The military had intervened. The leftists were waiting for the news in panic while the rightist had their trust in God. Shortly after the memorandum, detentions had begun. Most of the leftist leaders were rounded up and jailed since they were guilty of charges, and most of the Muslims were rounded up and arrested in order to strike a balance in the political arena... The 1960 coup was a movement controlled by the left. The 1971 Memorandum was moving along the same direction. However, Memduh Tağmaç and his friends seized the memorandum, and saved the memorandum from being under someone's control. The leftists who were not expecting such an attack from him were surprised. If the operation in March 8, 1971 was not stopped, the intervention would be very different. A "Revolutionary Constitution" would have come into effect and Turkey would have been a communist state; not by title but as a system... This was the common desire of the leftist and their revolutionary civilian mentors.

---

[7]  In his defense submitted by his attorneys to the 2nd State Security Court of Ankara, in the case he was accused of engaging in Nur activities, he stated, "I do not belong to any peculiar sects. I am only a Muslim. I declared many times that belonging to this or that movement means segregation. Other than being a Muslim, I do not belong to any movement. For that reason, I am not a "Nurcu"... and I am not a successor to anyone."

Hence, in the Ziverbey investigation, their true intensions were revealed and their disgustful thoughts came to light. The Memorandum was not a revolution or a coup. It is a warning to the government on certain matters. Naturally, it cannot be approved due its military nature. It is not possible to approve to bring down free will by force. However, we can look at this from a more positive perspective as it prevented a movement with worse consequences. I mean, it is bad, but compared to what's worse, it is not as bad."[8]

When the decision of the İzmir Military Court of Marital Law taken on September 20, was approved by the 3rd Military High Court, Gülen's punishment turned to conviction. After serving seven months in prison, he was freed with the amnesty law of the 37th administration of the Republic under Prime Minister Ecevit in 1974. It is interesting that although he spent seven months in prison, he did not lose his loyalty to the military. By not having an attitude against the "authority," Gülen showed the utmost respect to the 1971 Military Memorandum. Moreover, it is understood that the principle of "settling with the lesser of the two evils" is a principle that Gülen and his followers adopt not only in transitional periods but also in all critical times.

## The 1980 Coup

In the September 12, 1980 Military Coup, we encounter a different Fetullah Gülen. Gülen, known for his opposition to socialist movements, was very unhappy with the rise of leftist movements, and giving sermons about "losing religion" in 1979. Although Gülen glossed over the 1971 Memorandum

[8]  http://tr.fgulen.com/content/view/3500/128/

with some veiled criticism, he tried to pave the way to the 1980 Coup. This seems paradoxical, but it was indeed a result of a consistent strategy. It is a known fact that Gülen had enlarged his movement and his sphere of influence after the 1980 Military Coup. His closeness with the architect of the coup, Chief of Staff General Kenan Evren, prepared the ground for the community to overcome the coup without harm. Evren's positive opinions on moderate Islam is an important gain for Gülen. It is important to note that Evren's discourse on religion such as "The true religion is a pure religion, it is not obscurantism", "A nation without religion is unimaginable. We need to hold on to our religion tight"[9], "There is no way to divide people who have one God, one Quran, one prophet, and the same prayer...,"[10] coincides with the US's "Green belt and Islamization project". Let's read Gülen's statements in *Sızıntı* on July 1979, titled "Soldier," carefully. The article becomes more meaningful in the light of above mentioned information:

"In every nation's history, soldiers are highly esteemed... There is also a nation that are natural-born soldiers. He is born as a soldier, listens to military nursery rhymes and dies as a soldier. He is in love with the military, frontiers, struggle and raid. His bayonet had eased our wailing and pours water to our fire. We saw the heroism and the smiling face of the past in him many time in recent history. If he is not agile and does not stop the dark force from achieving the aim that has been in preparation for years, we could only cry cursing, as a nation, but could not do anything more ... Hail to aigrette, and let's pay homage to the flag, and to its esteemed holder."[11]

[9]    From Kenan Evren's speech on October 14, 1980 in Diyarbakır.
[10]   From Kenan Evren's speech on January 15, 1981 in Konya.
[11]   http://www.sizinti.com.tr/konular/ayrinti/asker.html

Gülen in his sermon in Bursa, on August 10, 1980, nearly one month before the coup, says the following:

"Precious Muslim, glorious dawn has already came. The rooster of that dawn had already began to crow. The buds have already sprouted. The scent of Prophet Muhammad has spread over Anatolia, the last bastion of Islam, the post which Turkish soldiers had protected with great effort. Perhaps I, and people like me will not be seeing this but many among you will see that divine light flow down from the sky..."[12]

After the September 1980 military coup,[13] although Gülen was on the wanted list, he did not hide his satisfaction with the coup. Before getting into his TV interview in 1995, let's read his article titled "Son Karakol," published in *Sızıntı* journal in 1985:

*"Hail to the Turkish Soldiers (Mehmetcik) who saved us when we lost our hopes..."*

"Military guard outposts are symbols of tranquility, peace and security. The order, serenity, and being alert against all dangers is the greatest guarantee for security and balance. Its chaos and crisis are big disasters for the nations. For many years, Anatolia served as a military guard out-

---

[12] Bulut, *Kim Bu Fethullah Gülen*, p. 365.
[13] After the 1980 Coup 650,000 thousand people were arrested. A total of 1,683,000 people were blacklisted. Through 210,000 court cases, 230,000 people were put on trial. As many as 7,000 people stand trial with capital punishment, while 517 were handed the capital punishment and fifty people were hanged. (Eighteen of them were leftists, eight of them were rightist, twentythree of them were criminals, and one of them was an ASALA militant.) The files of people persecuted with capital punishment were sent to parliament. As many as 908,440 people were put on trial for being members of illegal organizations. Some 30,000 people were fired as they were suspects. Fourteen-thousand people were expatriated, 30,000 people left the country as political refugees, 300 people died suspiciously, and 171 people died from torture. For more information, see Ahmet Şık, *Paralel Yürüdük Biz Bu Yollarda*, Postacı Publishing, Istanbul 2014, p. 59.

post for the land and the people whose life depended on it. I have no doubt that, in previous centuries, it had the most honorable duty of protecting the world's security and stability. Then later its flags had broken off one by one. However, with all its endurance it preserved its existence and survived. It guarded its essence and nobility despite changing and torn flags. Yes, throughout its history, many microbes had been spread onto it many times. His rose-bush like body has been shaken off hundreds of times, but it was never uprooted and beaten up. From reviving the Crusades mindset to infectious Jesuits tricks; each and every game to destroy this post and put its people to sleep has been tried by the foreigners. However, the expected outcome of our enemies was never achieved. The enemy has not been tired of inflictions, and the post has never been tired of saying "this life is always ready to be sacrificed for this purpose'…We cannot say that it has not been shaken off in this long struggle. This majestic tree has seen many falls and its majestic body has been renewed many times. However, it never fell down. Even at times the sky was darkened, and its body was stabbed many times, it never lost its hope. Its clock, with a national spirt, has a unique notion of time. The numbers on that clock could always be clearly read…

For centuries, against many paradoxes which tries to harm it, this legendary spirit remained stable and it always proved its impassability during the battles in Malazgirt, in Kosovo, and in the Dardanelles. Its majestic look continued to survive until a point when its roots had been attacked by the beast and inner enemies. After that day, this majestic pine tree has been burning from within and getting carbonated; it could not stand up well and renew itself. It got old. He has disloyal friends and cruel enemies. As poet Fuzuli said, '*Dost bî-pervâ, felek bî-rahm, devran bî-sükûn; Dert çok, hemdert yok, düşman kavi, tali'zebûn*' (Friends are disloyal, the world is miserable, the time is unstable. Problems are plenty, the enemy is strong, and the fortune is hopeless)... Right at the time when nightmares run rampant, the fifth column activities became widespread. Erotic thinking were disguised as innocent. Lust was made the most beloved commodity and the youngsters turned into a group of delirium. Yet, those who are connected to their spiritual roots were labeled as 'dogmatic' and 'formalist,' and the love of nation was considered to be shameful. Every day, a small group of people were writing pieces that were belittling and dishonoring our national spirit and making people run away from themselves, alienated from their own culture.

With all these happenings, innocent Anatolian people either waited with idiosyncratic patience and endurance or met this bizarre situation with simple tolerance in "silence". The condition of our poor "intelligentsia," which is the embodiment of spiritual misery and inferiority complex, was heart breaking. To them, anything done on the path to Westernization was a badge of honor for the Turks. These alienations forced assimilations and internal changes reached worrying degrees.

And now, the boat of the nation seemed to be like a boat that tottered and will be sinking soon. There were thousands of alien songs and there were thousands of drops of lethal wine on lips...Some are intoxicated with eroticism, some with libido, some appealed to existentialism, some are in love with insane delusions, some are changing their altars, running from one "God" to another. Right at this time, some alien hands started to transport these "hypnotized" souls with trains to their own land. A whole generation was in a mania, and they were invited to fake heavens like Hassan Sabbah's paradise!

Yesterday, we had inexperienced young men who were 'in love with Mehlika Sultan', now we have a crazy generation with blood on their hands, on their bosom, and on their clothes. These new generations know quite well what they are doing. Is there a need to find another external reason for the chaos and shambles? Isn't it normal for a generation that was not satisfied, that was left to its own devices to divide into different camps, and kill each other savagely...? Up until today, could we understand its collapse? Could we go down to the reasons for its degeneration? However, don't we need to be beside it like a guardian angel against the tyrants teaching them monstrosity? Alas..! We remained silent and were not irritated by the scenario of treachery that was staged... Yes, the whole nation, we watched it like we watch fights in the arenas and did not understand anything from this bloody struggle.

Those who realize the real face and violence of the staged game were the heroic watchmen of the last military outpost. They realized it despite the stage's fallacious vividness, frightening drowsiness of the ongoing waltz, and blinding effect of the costumes. This realization enables us to come to ourselves in our world of hope and understand ourselves. It is not appropriate to call it realization. It is a victory; it is catching the enemy tightly. This is the victory of cleansing and purifying social body from external impure ideas and practices, and turning it to pure form. This victory, if it brings all the expected outcomes, will occupy the supreme place in Turks' tab of victories. We saluted this intuition in a different article, and presented our gratitude to the house of our heroic veteran soldiers.

However, it was clear that a body that degenerates for years with thousands of different attacks, will not be healed immediately. There was a need for a more rooted, more sincere movement that would cleanse the national body from years of cancer... and now, in an abundant hope and joy, this last awakening that we consider the light of centuries-old longing, we see the existence of the last outpost as a sign of salvation. When our hopes dim, we wish our soldiers, who emerge as God's help for us to complete their mission and reach their goals."[14]

## The attempt to interpret coups

After the failed July 15 coup attempt, Gülen tried to tell global media that he is against the coup and for this reason he has nothing to do with the attempt in Turkey. Besides, he continuously mentions his loyalty to freedom and democracy. Gülen writes to persuade foreign media. However, Gülen's "previous rhetoric" gives him away. In a TV program on July 6, 1995, he said "it is not correct to find military interventions odd, it is not right to say that they are totally inappropriate..." Let's read Gülen's analysis on "business":

*"It is not correct to say that military interventions are inappropriate..."*

"However, under some circumstances, had the military not intervened, then that social gangrene could not have been healed, and the cancer could not have been cured. I know the processes that took Turkey to the 1971 Mem-

[14] http://www.sizinti.com.tr/konular/ayrinti/son-karakol.html

orandum. I was one of the people who faced injustices at those times. I know the 1980 coup very well too. I was a state official, and I was giving sermons. Everyone, as a slave of various ambitions, wanted to drag Turkey to different directions. And they very well may have succeeded in 1980. Turkey would have been thrown into the mouth of a dragon. And it could resemble other countries, such as those of Central Asia, which were under the tutelage of Russia, miserable, roguish and ruinous. For this reason, to judge military interventions in a negative way and label them as improper is not the correct attitude. However, couldn't military power overcome the anarchy and prevent chaos within the limits of democracy? Could it not eliminate terror? These will be analyzed by future sociologists and historians who will examine today's events, and publicly condemn the wrongdoers. History will condemn them too. For these reasons, I do not want to get into this subject..."[15]

We need to dwell on the fact that Gülen was on the wanted list after the 1980 coup but could not be or was not caught. Although Gülen said that he was "protected"[16] through "miracles", the reality was different. He states that, although he was on the wanted list, he was visiting his friends and allies at military barracks.[17] However, he does not explain the reasons and contents of those visits. It is highly likely that Gülen was not caught thanks to his strong links to the intelligence service. It is obvious that Gülen's complex web of relations with

---

[15] http://tr.fgulen.com/content/view/3178/132
[16] FG: "Along with my efforts to avoid getting caught, I felt that I was not caught intentionally. If they wanted, they could have caught me. The people who were searching for me did not seach from the heart. They did not look for me genuinely. While they were searching for me, I was even going to the military barracks and visiting friends. Interestingly enough, some commanders hung my photos on the walls of some barracks."
[17] Yeşilyurt, *Pensilvanya Canbazı*, p. 94.

state institutions and the deep state go back to the 1960s. His close relations with coup plotters after 1980 coincides with his setting up his cadres in public offices systematically. As Professor Ahmet İnsel puts it, he turns into "a monster that the state created".[18] We see that, although Gülen's structure within the state, which was effected, time to time, from the changing strategies of interim periods, largely completed its formation in the 1990s, and in the AK Party term, it had effective power in politics until 2010. But the claim that Gülen and his community became a dominant political actor is not true, as they were already powerful before the AK Party. When previous governments and prime ministers' positive opinions on Gülen are taken into consideration, it is a fact that with the exception of President Erdoğan, no other politician had the courage to dispute with Gülen. This analysis shows the amount of power granted to Gülen by previous politicians.

## Gülen and his community during the February 28 process

On February 28, 1997, Turkey experienced the last military intervention in recent history. It was different from other military interventions in terms of planning and structure. It resulted with the resignation of Erbakan, the end of the Refah-hYol coalition, and the formation of the "Batı Çalışma Grubu (Western Study Group)" that closely followed the activities of Islamic communities. For this reason, we see Gülen's attitude and behaviors of isolation from Islamic communities during this time quite very often. February 28 is an important breaking point for Gülen from other Islamic groups. Although Gülen was usually very sympathetic to the military and coups,

---

[18] *Taraf* newspaper, January 14, 2008.

he had difficulty in building dialogue with the military in the February 28 process. For example, he had close relations with pro-NATO soldiers in 1971 and 1980. But he was not able to communicate with nationalist soldiers after 1997, and that was, in a way, the beginning of the end for Gülen.

The records of various sympathetic actions that Gülen and his followers had carried out for the Deputy Chief of Turkish General Staff Çevik Bir in order to protect Gülenist businesses that provide financial means to the movement are still in the archives. It has been a matter of curiosity how Gülen – now presenting himself as defender of freedom and democracy to American public opinion – glossed over his letter to Deputy Chief of Turkish General Staff Çevik Bir, who, with the help of anti-democratic and the illegal Western Study Group labelled pious people as obscurantist. Actually, we know that Americans do not have sufficient information on Gülen from the statements of parents sending their kids to Gülen-affiliated schools. Before getting into the statements by Gülen that drive a wedge between him and Islamic communities, let's have a look the letter that Gülen wrote to Çevik Bir:

*"The Honorable Deputy Chief of Turkish General Staff, My Dear General..."*

"I ask your forgiveness and leniency as I will occupy your time on the matter of schools that are mentioned in the media lately, mistakenly attributed to my name.

I used the phrase 'schools that are mentioned in the media mistakenly attributed to my name'. Even Atatürk, a military, political and administrative genius, who built a state on the ruins of the Ottoman Empire, said, "My feeble body is going to be under earth one day, but the Turkish Republic will survive forever." In that regard, attributing all the success of the movement to this humble human being like me, who has no military, political and administrative genius, and "will be under the earth one day," would be an exploitation of the passion and hard work of our people, who are the main actors behind the success. That's why I said, "The schools were mistakenly attributed to my name."

As you know, and also attested by the founders and runners of these schools, I said time and again that my interest in those schools was limited to calling and encouraging people to establish such schools. I use them only as credit institutions – as some people would assume with their good intention – for the service of my country and state.

*My Dear Commander...*

As an honorable member of our heroic army and high echelon commander would know, especially in border cities like Kars, Erzurum, Ardahan, nationalistic sentiment is high as they have been invaded by the enemy many times. In a country that fought in World War I and the War of Independence, I was born right after World War II in an Eastern village that was under constant duress by the Soviets and raised in miseries. I tried to express the nationalist sentiment and my desire to serve my country as a Diyanet officer wherever I went, at every single mosque I prayed. At every opportunity that I found, I called on our people to serve our country, both in this life and the afterlife, without expecting anything in return, while I tried to bring to the surface the talents and love of the country and nation in our people. As the West developed with promotion of science and art starting from the Renaissance; and since the three reasons for our underdevelopment are ignorance, poverty and discursion, I called the community to educate their children, enlighten their minds with positive sciences, to eliminate superstitions and to protect our unity through loyalty to our state and its laws.

Some of the people that I had encouraged – when the state led the establishment of private schools – came together at various occasions and established schools in a competitive manner. After the institutions proved themselves successful in Turkey, similar schools were established in post-Soviet Turkic republics. Afterwards, they tried to open these schools in every corner of the world to lobby in favor of our country and ferment Turkish friendship.

If, there is any activity in any of these schools following the Turkish education curriculum, that are against the Republic of Turkey's secular, independent and social law state, before the Turkish state, I will encourage the closure of those institutions. If even a penny is taken from any foreign nation or any hostile institution – as some claim – I will end my diminishing life myself. In addition to this, our state can take over these schools that already belong to it, anytime it wants. Besides, since these schools already belong to our state, it is futile to mention such a transfer. As an honorable and elite member of our heroic army and as our Deputy Chief of Turkish General Staff, you can come and honor our schools and inspect them anytime, anywhere you like.

I apologize once again as I occupy your valuable time with such a letter and I propound my sincere respect to you. Fetullah GÜLEN"[19]

In the letter, Gülen tries to be as sympathetic as possible to Çevik Bir. It is clearly seen that Gülen appropriated the

[19] http://www.yenisafak.com/arsiv/2000/ekim/16/dizi.html

base motto of the army to create legitimization by saying "Its duty is to protect and watch for the Republic". Gülen, despite all his sympathetic behavior, could not convince the architects of February 28. Thus, approximately two years after the post-modern coup, he secretly left Turkey and settled in Pennsylvania. Due to its strategic structuring in the police force, Gülen's exit from the country was not difficult. It is not a coincidence that with the Ergenekon and Balyoz cases, *"Fetullah followers"* sentenced nationalist generals whom they labelled as *"residuals of February 28"*.

"Opposing coups" after the failed July 15 coup attempt, contradicts the present philosophy of the community, as Gülen supported Turkish democracy's disgraces of 1971, 1980 and 1997, applauded military interventions, and bowed respectfully to coup plotters. The statements Gülen made under the influence of the artificial fear created after February 28 on the decisions of National Security Council is noteworthy. Gülen made these statements on a TV show:

*"National Security Council's decisions are advices, but not memorandum..."*

"...When it is examined exogenously, some people may interpret it as a memorandum. I, personally, do not want to interpret it in this way. And there are certain reasons to not interpret it in that way. Rather than searching for its meaning in books, as a person who dealt with the 1971 Memorandum, I saw and experienced it. That memorandum was a memorandum. It was not like a series of advices. They eliminated the president, the prime minister, and the Cabinet, and transferred state power to something else. These people, even the ordinary people had seen what the memorandum meant. However, this time is different. People from the National Security Council, Ministry of Interior and Ministry of Foreign Affairs are there. The prime minister, head of the state, is there. They all sit down and talk among themselves. They discuss why Turkey is moving towards a crisis. They agree that there are some unsurmountable problems and there might be some worrisome issues in the future. As a result of these talks, they produced sets of advices. We call them recommendations. Everybody present there signs these recommendations, and a few of them signed it later. There might have been some considerations behind the idea of singing later as well... Rather than showing an attitude toward it, if we analyze it with the ideas of Jean-Jacques Rousseau, we may even call it the "Security Council Social Contract." Perhaps it is not the perfect name, but that is what actually happened. They all sat down together and discussed some issues and then signed a contract. From this perspective, I cannot compile the recommendations of the contract to be perceived as memorandum. I do not understand why it is emphasized in this way, and why the military is accused of giving a memorandum? I find this wrong."[20]

### *"National Security Council is a constitutional institution..."*

"Since the Republic and secularism was never under such threats until now, the segments responsible for protecting it are raising their voices. The National Security Council is a constitutional institution and it is their responsibility to take precautions and make recommendations on the matters they find dangerous in accordance with their "ijtihad." Even if their "ijtihad" is wrong, they would still earn a reward (thwab) for it. There is a great deal more to say on this matter. However, some segments of the society are

---

[20] Osman Özsoy, Mim Kemal Öke, Samanyolu TV, March 29, 1997.

not yet ready to accept it.... However, it is a fact that the situation of National Security is based on the Constitution. The National Security Council did not gain this privilege by surpassing everything, by surpassing laws, by surpassing the parliament, by surpassing the constitution. It did not come to that position by itself. I mean it does not pile decisions on people randomly. It is a constitutional institution. And a constitutional institution, whenever the constitution necessitates, does what is necessary...."[21]

*"The military wanted to solve the problems democratically..."*

"The military represents power. In places where power is represented, reasoning and judgment may not reach maturity at all times. Had the military wanted, it would have dictated their ideas. They would not have sat down and debated the issues for six hours. That means, in the presence of the head of the state, they debated the problem gently and conscientiously. And they presented their ideas and recommendations to everyone. They left the application of those recommendations to the government. That is to say, they wanted to solve the problem in a democratic way. They did not think of using anti-democratic measures. That's how I perceive the incident."[22]

## Resolution of March 1

Let's include another detail at this point. We know that, Gülen, who is always on the side of the power and authority, after the denied resolution on Iraq on March 1, 2003, sided with the

[21] http://fgulen.com/tr/turk-basininda-fethullah-gulen/fethullah-gulenle-tv-dergi-roportajlari/fethullah-gulen-televizyon-roportajlari/1463-Kanal-D-Kanal-Dde-Yalcin-Dogana-Verdigi-Mulakat
[22] Osman Özsoy, Mim Kemal Öke, Samanyolu TV, March 29, 1997.

US. Due to its importance, let's discuss this issue first, and then move the issue of headscarf.

As is known, the Turkish Parliament's rejection of the Iraq Resolution, for which the Turkish Armed Forces preferred to remain aloof, on March 1, 2003, harmed the US's interests to a great extent. We know from the consequences of the war that the US had a political, military and economic smack down as it was unable to use Turkish air space, ports and soil, and as it could not pull Turkey into a ground war. For these reasons, rejection of the resolution is an important breaking point in US-Turkey relations. The 'sack crisis' that followed the resolution showed how deep the fracture was. Up to a certain point, the crisis could be seen as a political fracture, and maybe considered normal in international relations. However, former Secretary of Defense Donald Rumsfeld preferred to define it as a "shame" in his book published by Penguin in 2012. "The American administration was sure. However, the Turkish Parliament did not approve the USA's demand to pass by a very small margin. Not taking the support of the key ally in region and a NATO member was a political shame as well as a serious problem for our military operations...."[23] If we look at the reaction of Rumsfeld, who was the mastermind of almost all of the hawkish politics of the time; and know the claims that General Chief of Staff Richard Myers threw his phone in the meeting with his Turkish counterpart, it is understood that the impact of this crisis in the White House was quite considerable. Another interesting detail is the fact that Gülen left Turkey with a green passport that was obtained through fake documentation. And when he got to Pennsylvania, he was able secure his permanent residency thanks to the bail of former Vice President of CIA

---

[23] Donald Rumsfeld, *Known and Unknown a Memoir*, Penguin Group, 2012, p. 78.

and Turkey specialist, Graham Fuller. Moreover, he continued his activities in a ranch under FBI surveillance during the 2003 crisis.

## Gülen's Take on the Headscarf

Gülen's efforts to use secular language on religious issues started before February 28. Gülen must have been informed about the military's large detailed work on obscurantism, that he felt the need to give speeches to mainstream media outlets. Gülen carefully selects his religious terminology as he would like to distance himself from other Islamic communities and the Welfare Party (RP) on matters concerning religion. Let's look at the cause of the fracture between Islamic communities and Gülen: his answer to the question "Should women cover their hair?"[24]:

*"The headscarf is a detail..."*

"The headscarf is not a matter of faith. These are not important matters in the general meaning of servitude to God. These are matters of secondary importance (Furu-at). The matters of faith were revealed to our Prophet in Mecca. There, prayer (salat) became an obligation for all Muslims in Mecca and later paying alms (zakat) also became obligatory. However, the veil is a little different. As far as I know, Muslim women were not wearing the headscarf until the 16th or 17th year of prophethood.

In principle, I think it is wrong to fight for details as we have more fundamental matters to resolve. Prioritizing these lesser issues would mean to de-emphasize the im-

[24] Headline of Ertuğrul Özkök's interview with Fetullah Gülen published in *Hürriyet* newspaper between January 23-28, 1995.

portance of the fundamental issues. I do not mean to say that people should continue their daily life, not cover their head, and then cover again after some time. The issue is not like this at all. First of all, it must be decided firmly where to put the matter of headscarf in religion. Another side of the matter is that, some people should not feel uncomfortable. It must be accepted in the social mosaic as one segment of the population."[25]

"...The headscarf issue had become a very sensitive matter in our schools. However, let me tell you this; what should a person do when she is stuck between schooling and not-schooling. Is it more beneficial for the nation and people to get an education, rather than not get an education? Is it necessary to be that much sensitive on a religious detail or is it better to use your preferences in a different direction? Everyone needs to judge with their own conscious and act accordingly. I personally think one should choose education".[26]

Gülen does not clarify, with his carefully selected rhetoric, whether or not there is an Islamic judgement on the veiling issue, which he does not regard as an issue of belief. He tries to create the perception that wearing the headscarf is a debated issue. The same Gülen criticizes people attending pro-headscarf protests on November 26, 1989 at İzmir Hisar Mosque. The protests, mainly supported, and to some extent organized by National Vision Movement (MGT) also get their share from Gülen's criticisms.

"Most of the women participating in the pro-headscarf protests are men in burqas. The rest are unveiled women

[25] Ertuğrul Özkök's interview with Fetullah Gülen published in *Hürriyet* newspaper between January 23-28, 1995.
[26] http://tr.fgulen.com/content/view/2257/141/

participating for provocation. Atheists and communists are behind these protests..."[27]

The explanatory statement by Gülen in 2013 on his website that tries to gloss his statements in the 1990s, is one of the best examples of Gülen's paradoxes. It is understood that Gülen is trying to gain back his lost prestige in the Islamic community by stating that veiling is openly commanded in the Qur'an. However, Gülen could not find the expected response from the Islamic communities. It is possible to interpret the statement that corresponds to the heydays of the AK Party-Jamaat conflict, on December 13, 2013, 16 years after February 28, as a major political cunningness by Gülen.

*"Hocaefendi had always said that veiling is God's command..."*

"For some reason, the word "furuat" (detail, or secondary importance) was taken out of context, and his preceding statements were disregarded. For example, he said, 'We do not have the right to have a say on veiling. There are clear unquestionable religious sources on the issue. This issue is beyond our interpretations. Because it is God's command. Veiling is not as important as the issue of faith." People ignored these statements and focused solely on the issue of "furuat." Moreover, Hocaefendi, never made a statement saying that veiling and wearing the headscarf are not duties of a Muslim woman, or never made a statement that it was an unimportant detail that was against the religion. On the contrary, he always stated that it was the command of God. However he always tried to set its level of importance in comparison to essential matters, and tried to state that it should not be a source of struggle among different segments of the society. In his explanation, along the lines

---

[27] November 26, 1989 sermon at İzmir Hisar Mosque.

with Muslim scholars who divided religious matters into two as theology (itiqad and faith) and practice (fiqh, furuat), and he referred to the issue of the headscarf as a matter of 'furuat'.[28]

Let's take a break from examining Gülen's paradoxical statements, and take a look at Dr. Tuğrul Keskin's interview with Betül Bozdoğan in 2014. Back then, Keskin was a faculty member at Portland University working on the community. Let's lend an ear to his important analysis:

*"Gülen uses democracy instrumentally..."*

"The community is a closed network, it is not transparent. It has a structure with its own intelligence and communication mechanisms. The aim of the community is not to struggle against corruption or democracy. They use democracy and corruption alone as an instrument against the opposition groups and people. They use corruption allegations as a leverage for their claims. It is known that Hizmet pays some American academics to write books on their movement. At the beginning of 2013, the community decided to pull some of its 'followers' abroad. For this reason, a group of people went abroad before December 17. It was a form of "hijrah" (migration) or struggle. That is to say, one could not help asking: Why does a social movement that claim to devote itself to service, act like a state?

Education institutions are just a facade of the movement. They are the ways by which they reach out to people in the regions they were established. The community's communication network is established thanks to the appointed members in each state in the US. That is to say, there are

---

[28] http://www.mynet.com/haber/guncel/gulen-basortusune-teferruat-de-di-mi-898284-1

regional representatives to whom these people are to report. Everyone reports every single meeting to their higher authorities on a regular basis. Interestingly enough, in every state the first place they visit is the FBI office. They publicize these visits on their websites, as they would like to establish themselves in the States. The community has two communication systems: the first one is an informal one like phones, emails, conversations; the other one that needs to be questioned is its unique and private web of communication. This web of intelligence uses high-tech communication programs. As we need to find the answer to the question of which community, the community also needs to declare to which one it belongs in an open democratic community.

The techniques that they use are mainly the same methods and procedures of American intelligence. The similar mechanism that the Department of Justice uses against the American Indian Movement and Black Panthers in McCarthy era are used in the Ergenekon and Balyoz cases and other similar cases. Does this have anything to do with Turkish policemen who were sent to the US for training purposes as of 1998?

The community or similar networks cannot afford to clash with Jewish and Israeli lobbies or criticize Israel. In fact, this lobby does not have a positive opinion of the community. According to them, the community is the better of the two evils compared to the AK Party. For this reason, especially after Gezi, some liberal Jewish circles had a honeymoon with the community. Do not forget, Israel is sacred for liberal and conservative Jewish groups. They do not criticize Israel's violation of human rights in Palestine as much as they criticize Turkey. The best example of this is the Jewish advisers of the Human Rights Watch. It is this cadre that criticizes Turkey most after the Gezi Park events".[29]

## Spiegel's criticism of Gülen

After Keskin's analysis, the article written by Maximilian Popp titled, "The Shadowy World of the Islamic Gülen Movement," is also important to show the paradoxes in Gülen's statements. Popp, tries to analyze the mysterious web of the relations of Gülen, "who is considered the Gandhi of Islam by his followers".

"People who have broken ties with Gülen and are familiar with the inner workings of this community tell a different story. They characterize the movement as an ultraconservative secret society, a sect not unlike the Church of Scientology. And they describe a world that has nothing to do with the pleasant images from the cultural Olympics... These critics say that the religious community (known as the "Jamaat" in Turkish) educates its future leaders throughout the world in so-called "houses of light," a mixture of a shared student residence and Qur'an courses. They describe Gülen as their guru, an ideologue who tolerates no dissent, and who is interested only in power and influence, not understanding and tolerance. They say that he dreams of a new age in which Islam will dominate the West. Some experts reach similar conclusions. Dutch sociologist Martin van Bruinessen sees parallels between the Gülen Movement and the Catholic secret society Opus Dei. American historian and Middle East expert Michael Rubin likens the Turkish preacher to Iranian revolution-

---

[29] *Star* newspaper, February 10, 2014.

ary leader Ayatollah Khomeini. According to a diplomatic cable obtained by WikiLeaks in 2010, US diplomats consider the Gülen Movement to be "Turkey's most powerful Islamist grouping". The Gülen Movement, the cable continues, "controls major business, trade, and publishing activities (and) has deeply penetrated the political scene". Most of Gülen critics abstain from disclosing their names. Because they are afraid of Gülen".[30]

---

[30] http://www.spiegel.de/international/germany/guelen-movement-accused-of-being-a-sect-a-848763.html

# CHAPTER VII
## JULY 15, 2016

# WAS GÜLEN EXPOSED AFTER JULY 15?

G ülen's statements after the failed July 15 coup attempt[1] changes one more time although previously he was consistently making positive references to coup attempts by saying, "It not correct to state that military interventions are totally bad".[2] Gülen, contrary to his usual calmness, makes statements in panic that denies the coup by saying "he supports the idea that elected governments should be changed within the democratic system". As a matter of fact, the reason behind Gülen's panic is obvious. The fact that some of the officers and privates who were caught on the coup night, gave Fetullah Gülen's name as the instigator; the demand of the soldiers who took Chief of Staff Hulusi Akar hostage so they could get him in touch with Gülen;[3] and the capture of the "imam of

---

[1] On the evening of July 15, 2016, Turkey experienced a bloody coup attempt. A group composed of senior officers and soldiers of the Turkish military, started the attempt in the early hours. We still do not know whether the aim of the coup plotters was to stage a coup or just to rehearse it. It is still riddle whether the main target was Turkey's democratic gains or President Erdoğan and AK Party cadres. After the attempt, there was a bitter balance sheet. On that night, Parliament was bombed 11 times, there were 246 martyrs, and 2,797 people were wounded. The attempt was clamped down with the determination of President Erdoğan, political party leaders, and the courage of the public that challenged the tanks. As a consequence of ongoing legal proceedings and administrative investigations, the mystery will revealed in the future.

[2] http://tr.fgulen.com/content/view/3178/132

[3] http://www.ntv.com.tr/turkiye/cumhurbaskanligi-sozcusu-kalin-karan-

the military," theologian Adil Öksüz at Akıncı Military Base, the coup's main military headquarters, and then his release, would make Gülen's flurry more meaningful. Opposing discourses like "Karun, pharaoh, dictator[4]" targeting President Erdoğan after 2013 should not be forgotten. The existence of concrete evidences, records of statements of the suspects showing that they got orders from Gülen and confessing soldiers' statements, prove that Gülen was the instigator of the bloody night of July 15. One detail needs to be noted here; through media, Gülen has been accusing President Erdoğan and the AK Party of authoritarianism. In Gülen's philosophy, this would be a sufficient reason to legitimize a "military intervention." We see Gülen's statements in which "he sees military interventions as a means for democratization" not only in the February 28 process, but also in 1971 and in 1980. Besides, Gülen does not feel the need to hide his attitude until July 15. Well, then what was the cause of the change in Gülen's rhetoric after the failed July 15 coup attempt? Of course the failure of the coup attempt... What would happen if the coup had been successful? Most probably, we could have seen how Gülen owned the coup, or attempted to develop an apologetic explanation for it.

Let's have a look at the statement he made to invite media members by accreditation at his ranch in Pennsylvania two days after the coup attempt, on July 17, 2016. The answers of the questions give us serious clues about Gülen's spiritual world. By the way, accredited journalists did not ask any question about his photographs with Adil Öksüz, who was caught at Akıncı Military Base on the coup night. This shows that the press conference was organized with handpicked journal-

lik-baslayan-gece-aydinlik-olarak-tarihimize,6qugeweFJkidrfrUxhexVg
[4]  www.herkul.org/herkul-nagme/391-nagme-egitime-darbe-plani

ists. Let's carefully read his statements that almost refute his past by saying "I never see military interventions under a positive light. Democracy cannot be sustained in this manner":

*"I do not know my followers..."*

*Do your followers have a role in the coup attempt in Turkey?*

As a matter of fact, I do not know all of my followers. There may be some sympathizers of what we are doing. I am telling with all my sincerity that I do not know even 1 percent of my followers; I do not know them, therefore I would not know if they have any role in the coup or not. Some people may have a distaste for some other people. Because of that they may develop sympathy toward others. This may be the Republican party, Nationalist party, or it may be you, it may be me.

*"I cannot say whether it is staged or not..."*

*In some media outlets, there are people who argue that the coup was staged by Erdoğan to increase his power within the military. What do you think?*

To say that it was staged will be like telling a lie, a slander for a believer. However if they based their claims on the past events, then I cannot say anything about that. These are events experienced in the past. Most of the times world leaders gained enemies in the past. There were also some assassination attempts for this reason. To say that they staged the coup would make us malignant like them. And I take refuge in God not to do such a thing.

*"I do not even know one-in-thousands..."*

*This morning, Secretary of State Kerry said: 'There is no extradition demand. If they have a proof on the matter, let them bring it on, then we can evaluate them.' What is your comment on this?*

There were prior demands like this. After December 17, December 25, they said 'his followers did it'. On that matter, I swear that I do not know even one in thousands among them. However, they may know me, humbly, people know me throughout the world. I am not a celebrity, I am an ordinary person. Sometimes you may be known due to the things you do, the things you write and sometimes you become involved in actions committed by friends and these things are ascribed to you. I mean they may know you. People in the Justice Department, or Security Forces may know you like this. I was here then. My opinion is that, first police seized the soldiers and then Justice Department people convicted them. I guess they have the military under their tutelage.

*"They made it seem like December 17/25 was the act of the community. This was not the case. It was defamation..."*

After that issue was finished, they began to talk about democracy, human rights, and the European Union. During the plebiscite, I encouraged friends from here. We were with them because of this. However, they did not want anyone next to them. Later on, they said people who have connections to you in the police and Justice Department did all this. They claimed that December 17/25 was the act of the community. This was not the case. It was a defamation act. As I refrain from slander and defamation earlier, I view this defamation with the same ugliness.

*"While they were anti-democratic, I declared that I was a Republican..."*

*Do you have any concerns about your everyday safety here? Do you have any concerns on the future of democracy?*

I do not have any concerns on my security in here. I

was staying in a small building previously, but then they warned me on the danger of fire. I guess the FBI had caught a person. I had a humble apartment there. Here I have a humble room, designed in accordance with my world view. Concerning democracy in Turkey, I want enlightened, open minded people to evaluate this from their perspective. Many years ago, in a panel I said 'democracy'. Then I was under attack by the media outlets that work with the current government. I said, "In fact, democracy is an irreversible process". I regard the Republic in the same manner. I declared that I was a Republican before they did. They were against democracy and the Republic back then. They were talking against secularism. However since they were the only ones on the matter, some people who like and respect them may vote for them. However, is there democracy in Turkey right now or not? What does this democracy promise for the future? I leave the answers to these questions to open minded, enlightened people.

*"I miss it, however, the truth is, most of the time, I feel like I staying here..."*

*Yesterday there was a moment in which it seemed like the coup attempt was successful. Did you think of returning back to your country at that moment? Would you have returned to your country, had the coup been successful? We know that you miss your country.*

I miss it, however, the truth is, most of the time, I feel like staying here. I did not get out of this building in the last two years. I live in seclusion. They do not interfere with me much. Hence, it is important not to interfere with people's freedom, freedom is very important for people, maybe freedom means people. In both Islamic and modern law, there are five or six things that need to be protected. One of these is freedom. I feel myself free here. I have seen coups, I have been divested. For these reasons, I had come here to the Mayo Clinic for treatment after February 28. Then the storm of June happened; they raised hell, and I was acquitted. And then I was in a fix. This is a clean environment, there are clean people around. To be honest, I was deserted, left alone with one or two friends here. However, I cannot say that I do not miss my country. However, probably, people prefer to stay in places where they are allowed to do things on their free will... Second, the coup plotters always put pressure on me. How will I know that they will not do the same? When I go, the same people may put me in prison. It is not safe. People do not like alternatives. The feeling we call jealousy and grudge may sometimes make people to do bad things that are even beyond heresy.

*"Personally, I was always against coups..."*

*Do you have any message for your former ally President Erdoğan and the Turkish public?*

Erdoğan will not accept my message. He regards it as an insult. Without clarifying the issue, he seems to charge the bill to us in last two days. I did not listen to him, but my friends did. For this reason, I think he will not accept even the kindest of my messages. I always pray to Allah to give guidance to him and myself. I will say to Turkish public, in the 1960 coup, I was an imam at a mosque in Edirne. I experienced that coup. They put me in jail during the 1971 Memorandum. Then I was acquitted at court. Later, after the 1980 coup, they followed me for six years and then they passed the verdict of non-prosecution. Again in 1997, during the event we call the storm of June, Nuh Mete Yüksel filed a claim against me. In the States,

I went to New Jersey and gave my testimony to a prosecutor. I was acquitted again. The High Court approved the decision. For this reason, as a man who suffered from coups, I can advise Turkish people not to have any sympathy for coups. I don't believe that coups will bring democracy, protect the Republic, and coups will not help Turkey integrate into the global world. For these reasons, I was always against coups. However, as you know the word coup has started to gain a new meaning in terminology. I do not care whether or not these people have been abused, corrupted or embezzled. However, they called the police and people from the Justice Department coup plotters, because they were giving them a hard time. There, they attributed that matter to us too. We are also against such coups. We do not want coups for anyone".[5]

Gülen's statements are not as simple as one communication expert may interpret. His statements hold "pathological" details that need to be interpreted by sociologists and psychiatrists. To avoid repetition, there is no need to comment on Gülen's statements. It is more beneficial to read the current analysis of a person who respected Gülen for many years. Fehmi Koru, the journalist who tried to be a mediator after December 17/25, is now convinced that Gülen has a sick soul. Let's read Koru, who finally has a clear judgement of Gülen:

*"Gülen is lying..."*

"...It is clear where I will take this conversation. In Pennsylvania to me, at CNN to Zakaria... The same denial. Today I can connect the statements he made two days ago to Fareed Zakaria from CNN and many media outlets saying 'I have no connection with this coup", with his state-

[5] http://www.voanews.com/a/fethullah-gulen-/3421616.html

ment after the December 17 attempt that targets the government saying, "We have nothing to do with these, Mr. Fehmi"… I guess he is deceiving himself, his denial is not a 'lie' to him….

In our meeting with Gülen in Pennsylvania, there was another person to testify our conversation. Despite this, Gülen said that I had misreported our conversations in my writings. I think that the same self-deception is at work here again."[6]

## How did Michael Rubin know about the coup attempt three months ahead?

To see the big picture more clearly, let's move to another detail. Let's read the article written by Michael Rubin, who we know through his apologies to Gülen and his community, published on the American Enterprise Institute's website, arguing, "*A probable coup attempt in Turkey, contrary to what is believed, will strengthen democracy but not authoritarianism*":

> "*Could there be a coup in Turkey?…*"

"The situation in Turkey is bad and getting worse. It's not just the deterioration in security amidst a wave of terrorism. Public debt might be stable, but private debt is out-of-control, the tourism sector is in free fall, and the decline in the currency has impacted every citizen's buying power. There is a broad sense, election results notwithstanding, that President Recep Tayyip Erdoğan is out of control. He is imprisoning opponents, seizing newspapers left and right, and building palaces at the rate of a mad sul-

---

[6] http://fehmikoru.com/cemaat-icinde-derin-cemaat-var-derdim-bugun-artik-di-yemiyorum-sebebi-su/

tan or aspiring caliph. In recent weeks, he has once again threatened to dissolve the constitutional court. Corruption is rife. His son Bilal reportedly fled Italy on a forged Saudi diplomatic passport as the Italian police closed in on him in an alleged money laundering scandal.

His outbursts are raising eyebrows both in Turkey and abroad. Even members of his ruling party whisper about his increasing paranoia which, according to some Turkish officials, has gotten so bad that he seeks to install anti-aircraft missiles at his palace to prevent airborne men-in-black from targeting him in a snatch-and-grab operation. Turks — and the Turkish military — increasingly recognize that Erdoğan is taking Turkey to the precipice. By first bestowing legitimacy upon imprisoned Kurdish leader Abdullah Öcalan with renewed negotiations and then precipitating renewed conflict, he has taken Turkey down a path in which there is no chance of victory and a high chance of *de facto* partition."

The most important part of Rubin's article is hidden in his statements like "Turkey is on the verge of a civil war" and "how a probable coup will be perceived in the West and in the US". Let's continue to read what Rubin said on March 21, 2016:

*"If Turkish military moves to oust Erdoğan..."*

"After all, if civil war renews as in the 1980s and early 1990s, Turkey's Kurds will be hard-pressed to settle for anything less, all the more so given the precedent now established by their brethren in Iraq and Syria. Erdoğan long ago sought to kneecap the Turkish military. For the first of his rule, both the US government and European Union cheered him on. But that was before even Erdoğan's most ardent foreign apologists recognized the depth of his descent into madness and autocracy. So if the Turkish military moves to oust Erdoğan and place his inner circle behind bars, could they get away with it?

*"On the event of a probable coup, the US would continue to work with the new regime..."*

In the realm of analysis rather than advocacy, the answer is yes. At this point in election season, it is doubtful that the Obama administration would do more than castigate any coup leaders, especially if they immediately laid out a clear path to the restoration of democracy. Nor would Erdoğan engender the type of sympathy that Egyptian President Mohamed Morsi did. When Morsi was ousted, his commitment to democracy was still subject to debate; that debate is now moot when it comes to the Turkish strongman. Neither the Republican nor Democratic frontrunners would put US prestige on the line to seek a return to the *status quo ante*; they might offer lip service against a coup, but they would work with the new regime. Coup leaders might moot European and American human rights and civil society criticism and that of journalists by immediately freeing all detained journalists and academics and by returning seized newspapers and television stations to their rightful owners. Turkey's NATO membership is no deterrent to action: Neither Turkey nor Greece lost their NATO membership after previous coups. Should a new leadership engage sincerely with Turkey's Kurds, Kurds might come onboard.

*"Neither European nor the American public opinion would likely be sympathetic to the execution of Erdoğan..."*

Neither European nor the American public opinion would likely be sympathetic to the execution of Erdoğan, his son and son-in-law, or key aides like Egemen Bağış and Cüneyd Zapsu, although they would accept a trial for corruption and long incarceration. Erdoğan might hope friends would rally to his side, but most of his friends — both internationally and inside Turkey — are attracted to his power. Once out of his palace, he may find himself very much alone, a shriveled and confused figure like Saddam Hussein at his own trial. I make no predictions, but given rising discord in Turkey as well as the likelihood that the Turkish military would suffer no significant consequence should it imitate Abdel Fattah el-Sisi's game plan in Egypt, no one should be surprised if Turkey's rocky politics soon get rockier".[7]

When Rubin's connection with Gülen and his followers is taken into consideration, it will not be wrong to say that he is trying to manage perception about a possible coup attempt in Turkey. It cannot be known whether his article is a manifestation of Gülen's statement, "If our narration of an issue will create some reactions in some people's conscious, we must let one other person narrate the incident by saying 'The right of the Truth is above everything'..."[8] However, is it possible to justify how an American researcher writing such a daring and assertive article, just before a bloody coup attempt, as "brainstorming"... Rubin's article dating three months after July 15 raises questions as it writes "It has now been almost three months since the failed coup in Turkey. The events of July 15 were predictable, but they nevertheless mark a watershed in modern Turkish history. Still, it would be a mistake to view the coup as a single event. Turkey actually experienced two coups, but it will be the third and coming coup which

[7] https://www.aei.org/publication/could-there-be-a-coup-in-turkey/
[8] Fethullah Gülen, *Asrın Getirdiği Tereddütler 3*, Nil Publishing, İzmir 1985, pp 166-177.

could be the most violent and might very well cost Turkish President Recep Tayyip Erdoğan his life."⁹ Lastly, Rubin's article, dated November 3, 2016, "Turkey will be a blood bath" is important to understand who sets plots for Turkey:

*"Erdoğan is getting ready for a bloodbath..."*

"Turkish President Recep Tayyip Erdoğan called the failed July 15 coup attempt a "gift from God." The Turkish government immediately blamed Erdoğan's former ally-turned-rival Fetullah Gülen for being behind the plot, the genesis of which remains unclear, but the simple fact is that none of the material Turkish officials have given to their US counterparts has yet risen to the standard of proof — let alone credible evidence — to support Erdoğan's charges. It is noteworthy that the Turkish press purports to describe the US reaction as accepting of the Turkish material, yet no American officials have ever been quoted as saying anything near what the Turkish press describes. Indeed, alternate narratives about the July 15 coup attempt are equally compelling.

The only certainty is that the attempted coup became the excuse Erdoğan needed or crafted in order to purge those opposed to or insufficiently enthusiastic about his agenda. Much of what has been reported in the Western media has focused on the ongoing purge of teachers and university professors. Certainly, there is a newsworthy irony to a man whose university diploma appears to be forged assuming the right to appoint university presidents through a board he has staffed with his cronies. But it is what Erdoğan has done in recent days to the police which should put chills down the spines of those who care about Erdoğan's intent and Turkey's future.

---

⁹  https://www.aei.org/publication/the-next-phase-in-turkeys-political-violence/

Last week, Erdoğan appointed new police chiefs for 61 out of Turkey's 81 provinces. He also assigned 55 police chiefs to central departments that act as police professional bodies. (On page 105 of his book, Turkish academic and counter terrorism specialist Ahmet Yayla explains how these positions relate to Turkish counterterrorism). Some of the police chiefs Erdoğan fired were religious and some even supported him. None were followers of Gülen, simply because those who were had long ago been purged. Most of the chiefs whom Erdoğan has appointed are fiercely nationalist, very young, and relatively inexperienced, and so are likely to more easily defer Erdoğan's orders. The problem seems not that Erdoğan believed all the sacked chiefs disloyal — most were not and many he had appointed in the first place — but rather that he considered them soft, unwilling to use the extreme violence Erdoğan believes will be necessary to exert not only on Turkey's Kurds but also many liberal or apolitical Turks as he moves to further consolidate control.

Throw into the mix that Erdoğan has also just in the past few days extended the time for which Turks can be detained without access to an attorney to six months. What this sets the stage for is a significant augmentation of torture in custody in order to extract forced confessions, a practice that has become more common since July. Erdoğan's ruling party has also begun issuing weapons permits to loyalists, especially through the Ottoman Youth Authority (Osmanli Ocaklari). I have previously reported Erdoğan's appointment of former general Adnan Tanrıverdi, the head of SADAT, to be his military counsel. Tanrıverdi had been dismissed by the Turkish General Staff during the 1997 soft coup and appears bent on revenge against the secular order. SADAT which has trained paramilitaries and Special Forces, is increasingly becoming Erdoğan's Islamic Revolutionary Guard Corps. Indeed, SADAT appears to have been behind much of the killing of civilians which Erdoğan's media blamed, absent any evidence beyond forced confessions, upon Gülenist coup plotters.

All this hints at Erdoğan's long game. He appears to be consolidating his own religious control through the Service for Youth and Education Foundation of Turkey (TURGEV, a charity on whose board Erdoğan's son sits) and Hayrettin Karaman, Erdoğan's favorite local Islamic leader.

But, as Erdoğan seeks to change the constitution, he also wants to win through the point of a gun what he cannot win popularly. The issue at hand is not simply the Turkish public — Erdoğan believes he has them cowed — but rather Doğu Perinçek, a former Maoist and ultranationalist. Perinçek has been the chief beneficiary of Erdoğan's purges, as they have eliminated many of his opponents as well. Today, Perinçek is effectively the shadow defense minister. He has said he will not allow the constitutional change which means the terms of the showdown are now clear.

Whomever wins, the only certainty is that Turkey is headed for a bloodbath. The only questions are how soon it comes, and whether Erdoğan is more prepared than Perinçek".[10]

Rubin's emphasis on Perinçek is noteworthy. It is seen in the article that Perinçek's name is highlighted as a figure that dominated the deep state apparatus. However, it should be

[10] Michael Rubin, "Erdoğan prepares for a bloodbath", https://www.aei.org/publication/erdogan-prepares-for-a-bloodbath/

noted that Rubin's analyses are far from reality. For this reason, to whom this researcher, with all these irrational analyses serve and which perception operation he is part of in will be clear in the near future.

A former FBI officer, Sibel Edmonds, who was on a TV show on July 18, sheds light on the dark relations between Rubin and Gülen:

"To me, this is a coup rehearsal, in which Gülen was used as a tool, that was supported by CIA-NATO. I mean, it was just a warm up exercise. A real coup against Erdoğan is on the way. Probably, what happened on July 15 was a trial to see whether people will oppose the coup or not."[11]

## İlker Başbuğ's comment on July 15

Another name that points to Gülen's connections in the intelligence is former Chief of Staff İlker Başbuğ. Başbuğ, who spent twenty-six months in Silivri Prison after the Ergenekon case, thinks that Gülen is openly collaborating with the CIA. Başbuğ, turning his interview with Ahmet Hakan after July 15 in to a book, argues that after the December 17/25 events, President Erdoğan was left alone in his fight against the Gülenists. Başbuğ's statements arguing that Gülenist officers were behind this coup, holds important details to understand the level that Gülenists reached in the Turkish Armed Forces. Let's read Başbuğ's statements:

*"Erdoğan fought alone against the community..."*

"The main culprit behind the July 15 attempt was the community that had planned, managed, and orchestrated

---

[11] http://www.boilingfrogspost.com/2016/07/18/newsbud-sibel-edmonds-dissects-the-turkey-coup-attempt-a-cia-gulen-concocted-dry-run/

it. Secondly, the other responsible parties were the ones who did not do what they were supposed to do at once, or the ones who hesitated to take actions against the attempt ... Are these people members of the community? No. There is a group like that among them. There may be some people, although they are not from the community, who would like to take advantage of the situation.

I do not consider July 15 as a military intervention. July 15 is an armed rebellion of the Jamaat that infiltrated the Turkish Armed Forces. July 15 is not in the same category as in all other previous coups. The planners and perpetrators of July 15 is the Jamaat. The people who were late to interfere in this may not all be from the Jamaat. Efforts are made to make it appear as the coup originated from the Turkish Armed Forces. Previously, we expelled Gülenists with intelligence acquired from the National Intelligence Organization (MİT). After 2002, we did not receive such reports, even for a single person. The MİT was disconnected from the Turkish Armed Forces as its undersecretary become civilian. The Turkish Armed Forces cannot surveillance soldiers outside of the barracks, the MİT should do that. The Turkish Armed Forces does not have enough resources to track down FETÖ.

The community's infiltration of the Turkish Armed Forces goes back to the 1970s. The real consolidation of power of the Jamaat happened during Turgut Özal's years. Bülent Ecevit also has sympathy for them. It was like that also during Tansu Çiller's times. We see that Erbakan keeps his distance from the Jamaat. 2002-2007 is another period. It is the period of let's have good relations with the Jamaat, but avoid clashing with the Turkish Armed Forces. While I was the Chief of General Staff, I warned people by saying, 'it is a threat for us today, but maybe for you tomorrow.' My arrest was a message for some people. The message was for the Prime Minister. A month later, on February 7, the MİT incident broke out. We see that the AK Party and the Jamaat came to a point of disengagement. Between 2012-2016, Erdoğan fought against the Jamaat alone. On July 15, people in command did not do a good job. Some scenes of privates and officers were disturbing. The investigation of July 15 may be delegated to an independent institution.

The Jamaat was going to establish a state based on its religious doctrine. The target here was the Turkish Armed Forces. The coup attempt also got support from abroad. Not having any support abroad is against the nature of things. Where does Gülen live? In the USA. Who provides him with all these opportunities? The CIA did. Did the CIA give him permanent residency for nothing? Do you really think that intelligence would not use him? With their frames, the Turkish Armed Forces did not lose its prestige but its power."[12]

### What is he afraid of?

Turkey's diplomatic insistence on Gülen's extradition can be the beginning of the end for Gülen and his followers. However, it does not seem rational to expect American intelligence to deport someone with whom they have secret and dirty relationship for a very long time based on an "Extradition Agreement". Although Gülen is aware of this situation, he seemed to be restless in his statements after July 15. However, Gülen, who promotes himself as "The insurance of moderate Islam

---

[12] İlker Başbuğ, *15 Temmuz Öncesi ve Sonrası*, Doğan Publishing, Istanbul 2016.

in an era which radical Islam is on the rise", sends messages to the White House and American media through different means. We know from American media sources that to build an image of "a wise man", Gülen spent a large sum of money and sustains his relations with American congressmen. Because of that his schools were under FBI investigation.[13] As this is the case, even a small reaction in American public opinion may mean the beginning of the end for Gülen and his followers. For this reason, Gülen is always very cautious. It is not hard to understand, with what kind of a psychology he wrote his *New York Times* article. In the article, Gülen demanded that the American government not extradite him. He said "Throughout my life, I publicly and privately denounced military interventions in domestic politics... I have been always advocating for democracy for decades.....I would never want my fellow citizens to endure such an ordeal, as someone who would get harmed, who was repressed and who was sent to prison by military regimes. If someone who appears to be a Hizmet sympathizer has been involved in an attempted coup, he betrays my ideals...."[14] Gülen tried to deny his connection with the senior officers who were caught or made confessions. It is a fact that his statements are futile. It must be the result of his despair to think that Turkish people will believe someone who adopted a supportive stance in all three previous coups on the side of the military, with all these "concrete evidences".

It may seem like an advantage for him that the American public does not have enough knowledge on his past. However, it is a mystery for how long he will keep his past as a secret at a time in which all spot lights turned on him. Former

---

[13] http://odatv.com/fbidan-fethullah-gulen-sorusturmasi--2709131200.html
[14] *The New York Times*, July 25, 2016, Fethullah Gulen: I Condemn All Threats to Turkey's Democracy.

Pentagon speaker and Foreign Affairs adviser Jeffrey D. Gordon thinks that Turkey is right on her claims about Gülen. It seems like Gordon's analysis will trigger a reaction in the American public opinion in the future. Let's read what Gordon wrote in *The Hill* magazine in December 2015:

*"Turkey is fully right in asking Gülen's extradition..."*

"Washington and Ankara should agree on extraditing a U.S.-based Islamist leader who presents a danger to each capital. This month a Turkish court issued arrest warrants for cleric Fetullah Gülen and 66 others for allegedly operating a secretive, cult-like parallel government within politics, police and the judiciary. According to the Turks, the Gülen Movement is conspiring to topple the democratically elected government of President Recep Tayyip Erdoğan and install an Islamic theocracy, similar to the harsh system of government in Iran.

*"The last thing that Turks need is a secret power that is set to destroy their government..."*

Ironically, this organization is being directed from the land of the free – or more specifically, from Pennsylvania's Pocono Mountains, where Gülen is residing in exile. Though he has lived there since 1999, his weekly online sermons and network of roughly 3-6 million followers are setting off alarm bells from Istanbul to Ankara.

Turkey appears on high alert for external and internal threats because it hasn't been this vulnerable in generations. The nation of 75 million and NATO's second largest military is challenged by a terrorism epidemic; close to 2.5 million Syrian refugees with more on the way; and a renewed spike in violence with the Kurdish militants of the PKK, also known as the Kurdistan Workers' Party. The latter conflict has already killed 40,000 since the 1970s. The last thing the Turks need is a stealth force attempting to sink their government – from the US of all places.

*"The Gülen Movement is already degenerated..."*

So why should Americans care? Well, beyond supporting an important treaty ally, considering the rising tide of religious extremism penetrating both sides of the Atlantic, the last thing Americans need is people indoctrinating our citizens and recently arrived refugees into the merits of theocracies. Moreover, legitimate questions about U.S. immigration and security policies shouldn't be simply met with allegations of "Islamophobia" and "xenophobia," including from some well-intentioned people who perhaps haven't looked into the details. Though the Gülen Movement has stayed mostly under the radar, their American taxpayer-funded network of 120 charter schools throughout the country is the largest nationally. But it's not just preaching ideas that promote extremist thought, including second class status of women and girls, it's also terribly corrupt. The FBI has been investigating numerous Gülen-linked schools for various allegations of improper use of public financing, while their shady immigration, contracting and salary practices for thousands of imported young male teachers have also raised questions in local communities.

*"It is not surprising to see them donating one million dollars to the Clinton Foundation..."*

Where there's a perfect storm of corruption, indoctrination and proselytization, the next logical step is to reach out to top US politicians for building support. Thus it is not surprising that Gülen Movement followers have reportedly donated up to one million dollars to the Clinton Foundation. Plus they've operated non-profit shell groups which have arranged and paid for as many as 200 trips to Turkey for members of Congress and staffers since 2008 including Reps. Mike Honda (D-Calif.), Bob Filner (D-Calif.) and Mo Brooks (R-Ala.). According to a *USA Today* investigation this year, those trips apparently violated Congressional rules repeatedly and may have broken federal laws.

Gülen is now being sued at a US District Court for a "campaign of persecution against a different religious group" and "arbitrary and prolonged detention" of between 8-20 months. This includes allegations of "abuse of the US immigration system." Again, no surprise.

*"We do not need people and organizations that use religion..."*

Considering it is hard enough to keep our country safe after the terrorist attacks of 9/11, Boston Marathon, Ft. Hood, Chattanooga and San Bernardino, we don't need any help from individuals and organizations manipulating religion to build a personal cult. The same goes for Europe. We must increase collaboration with allies to stop increasingly common terrorist attacks. In fact, the Turkish government had warned France twice about one of the Paris attackers, a French citizen who helped kill 89 people at the Bataclan Concert Hall last month. Yet nothing was done.

*"Fetullah Gülen should be extradited..."*

The lesson is clear: Americans and Europeans must act on credible intelligence about extremists in our midst and take decisive action. Fetullah Gülen and his inner circle should be extradited and face the music in Ankara. Based on their actions, it simply appears they're attempting to use religious garb to cloak criminal behavior. The White House and Congress ought to see right through that and we should send them packing".[15]

## What does Gülen's extradition file include?

Turkey insists that Gülen is the mastermind behind the July 15 coup attempt. Because the prepared file consists of concrete evidences of witnesses and suspects against Gülen. Although, some Gülenists say the file said was prepared under pressure, the facts are evident. Turkey explicitly states in the file it sent to the American Justice Department that Gülen is the person behind the putsch. For this reason, Turkey demands Gülen's arrest for six different charges, and demands his extradition. In the file, Gülen is accused of "Murder in the first degree, the assassination attempt on the president, the attempt to destroy the constitutional system, the attempt to destroy the parliament and hinder its functioning, the attempt to abolish the Republic of Turkey and hinder its proper functioning and the establishment of armed terrorist groups".

Let's analyze Chief of Staff General Hulusi Akar's statement on the file, sent to the US, stating that Gülen was the one behind the putsch:

"I believe that the coup plotters are members of an organization. I believe that the terrorist organization understood that our detailed and serious works of the August Meeting will harm the terrorist organization severely, and this is a very important triggering factor in the coup at-

[15] http://thehill.com/blogs/congress-blog/homeland-security/264031-turkey-justified-in-seeking-extradition-of-us-based

tempt. Besides, together with vice president, we had developed some suspicion that some personnel around us were linked to this terrorist organization. We were going to take some very serious steps in the meeting. Another reason that pushed the terrorists in this direction is the developments in investigations and files on the terrorist group and the distance that all governmental institutions placed against the terrorist group. I am pressing charges against every single person who is a member of this terrorist organization, who harmed me, my nation, my comrade in arms, members of the security forces, government institutions, Turkish history and Turkish civilization".[16]

"The terrorist organization" that is mentioned by General Akar is the Gülenist Terror Group (FETÖ) that is also included in the "red book" of the National Security Council. The parts in which General Akar states that the coup plotters demanded "to get the general in touch with Gülen" on the night of July 15, does not beg any further interpretation. Let's continue to read Akar's record of testimony:

"The struggle of our state against FETÖ/PDY is also a struggle that we take part in with maximum precision and care. This year in our August Meeting we were preparing a plan that would strike this organization very harshly. At that point, I think that the organization had learned about this plan and they attempted a coup with unthinkable cruelty and craziness, and killed civilians, bombed Parliament, attacked their own military and troops, and bombed security units. While we were reaping successful results against the separatist terrorist organization in the southeast of Turkey, with the help of security forces, gov-

---

[16] From the July 15 record of statements.

ernors, mayors, the Justice Department, intelligence services and the armed forces, we had this nefarious attack on our country. This despicable act is going to remain a black stain on our history forever".

It is clearly understood from Akar's following statements that Fetullah Gülen is the instigator and perpetrator behind the putsch. Statements by the other officers who confessed strengthen Akar's claims. However, the West's allegations that the statements, including Akar's, were given under pressure and torture, reveal their prejudice and bias on the matter. Let's continue to read Akar's statements:

*"Sir, the operation is starting, we will capture everyone.*
*Battalions, and brigades are on their way..."*

"Because of the source of the information, we took it seriously. Yaşar Pasha, the commander of the Land Forces, Salih Zeki Çolak, and I started to debate the necessary precautions and measures at once. Immediately I gave my orders, after meeting with SKKHM, for all military planes and helicopters in the air to land down not just in Ankara but throughout Turkey, and not to let any planes or helicopters take off until further command. Second Command-in-Chief Yaşar Güler transmitted this order to the Air Force Command and Control Center. In terms of confirming the information received from the MİT and, to clear the matter in regards to the likelihood of the concretization of the flight operations stated in the information, with the quickest and most effective measure required, I immediately ordered the Land Forces commander to do what is necessary. I asked the General Staff to take personnel from the Central Command Headquarters and Judiciary to go to the Military Aviation School and solve the issue and take necessary judicial and administrative precautions immediately. I also ordered them to update me as soon as they arrive at the school.

In our analysis of the situation we discuss that the incoming information may be part of a bigger plan. So we did not confine ourselves to just the above mentioned precautions. I called the Ankara Garrison Commander General, and ordered him to go to the Etimesgut Armored Unit personally and to prevent any tanks or armored vehicle from leaving the unit. Our meeting had ended as we had taken the preliminary precautions... Dişli, while sitting on one of the chairs by the table, said "Sir, the operation is starting. We will take everyone. Battalions and brigades are on their way. You will see soon". He seemed to be very excited and very different from the mood I was accustomed to. I could not make sense of his mumblings at first. Then I understood that he was talking about a coup. I became angry, and said, "What the hell are you talking about? What operation? Are you crazy? Don't even dare!" Since I was facing away from the door, I am not sure whether the door was open or not.

*"Sir, it is over..."*

I asked the whereabouts of the second commander-in-chief and the other commanders. Dişli maintained, "Take it easy, they will come." Naturally, I was very upset. I tried to convince them that "They were making a very big mistake; they were going to be in a big trouble; they were going to be punished for that; they should not drag everyone into this quagmire; and they should end this without violence and death." But I was unable to convince them. Trying to keep his cool, he was saying things which could mean, 'Sir, it is over, and everyone is one their way now.' At some point, Dişli walked out the door. When I turned to the door, I saw

Captain Serdar, Non-Commissioned Officer Abdullah, and Lieutenant Colonel Levent. I also realized that there were other fully-equipped personnel from the Special Forces.

When they all attempted to enter the room, I stood up. Levent Türkkan was shouting at me, "Sir, sit down. Don't stand up. Take it easy." Someone pushed me to sit down in the chair. In the meantime, another person gagged me with a hand towel, and did not allow me to breath. He also wrapped his arms around my neck. I was struggling to breathe. While I was struggling to free my nose to breathe, someone else handcuffed me. After this, they gagged me even tighter, allowing me to breathe only through my nose. It was obvious that they did not want me to yell. Once I caught my breath a little, they removed the cloth from my mouth. Since my wrists were badly hurt during the struggle, I began to scream again. I asked them to remove the handcuffs, and stood up. Levent Türkkan once again told me to sit down, and said, "Sir, take it easy, otherwise, I am going to shoot you." I took two steps towards him and shouted "Shoot!" I saw the robotic hesitation between shooting and not shooting in his eyes. Meanwhile, I demanded them to release me from the handcuffs. I guess with the consent of Mehmet Dişli, they took out a commando knife. It was a blind knife. One of the soldiers tried to cut the handcuffs off, but could not do it. Hence, I got angry again and shouted. They tried for the second time and cut off the handcuffs. They made me sit with a soldier behind me, debilitating me in this way.

A considerable time passed. Although the TV was on, and I was hearing plane and gun noises, there was no such news on the TV. Later, the news started to be broadcasted about the soldiers blocking the road on Bosporus Bridge.

They all waited cold bloodedly and silently, without saying a word. And after some time they said "We are going!" and took me with them. I wanted my briefcase, hat and jacket. My cellphone was left in the adjutant's room. I guess they handed me my jacket and hat. They said they would bring the suitcase later.

*"All the guns were pointing at me in the helicopter..."*

One of the soldiers was pointing an automatic gun at me, walking backwards. I shouted again and angrily said, "What the hell are you doing?"... I repeated several times that I have my glasses in the briefcase. However, they did not bring the suitcase. The helicopter took off. They did not tell me where we were heading. I did not ask. All the arms in the helicopter were pointing at me. Mehmet Dişli was on the helicopter too. After flying for some time, we landed. I asked them where they took me. They told me that it was the Akıncı Base and they put me in a minibus and took me to a building. I was in shock both because of this situation and with the presence of Akın Öztürk in the building. I asked him what he was doing there. He said he came there with his wife and the commander of Land Forces. They came there from İzmir with a plane belonging to the commander post. He said he came here upon a phone call from Abidin Ünal while he was at his daughter's house. In fact, he also said he was trying to tell this to them, but they were not listening to him. I told him the same thing that I have been saying since the start of the incidents. I also saw Admiral Ömer Harmancık and General Hakan Evrim. I said the same things I had said before; that they had lost their minds, they were making a mistake and this could not be happening in this era. I said things like "Don't you see Syria and Egypt?" "Don't you know how these incidents take us back decades?" They did not care at all.

*"If you like we can put you in touch with our opinion leader Fetullah Gülen..."*

He said 'Sir, read this. If you sign and read this on TV, everything will be fine. We are taking everyone, we are bringing in everyone". I intensely and angrily refused the offer. I yelled at them saying "Who do you think you are? Who are you? Where are the people you said you are bringing in? Where is the Second Commander in Chief? Where are the ministers? Bring everyone you have. Who is your leader?" Then Hakan Evrim said something like, "If you like we can put you in touch with our opinion leader Fetullah Gülen". I scolded him saying that" I will not be meeting with anyone". Everyone left the room but Akın Öztürk. I guess that we went into the base commander's room around midnight. I was saying the same things to Akın Öztürk Pasha. He was telling me things like they are not listening to him either. Sergeant Abdullah remained in the room for some more time. As far as I remember, there was another person who I think might be the adjutant of the Base Commander. When they wanted me to sign and read the memorandum, I did not even touch it. I did not read it. I listened cynically as they were reading it to me. The people in the room were leaving and coming back. Akın or another person told me that there was another room that was in use as the operation center, and there were 30-40 people in there. I did not see the other room. I stayed in the same room throughout the whole time I was held hostage.

*"President's address dashed all hopes of the coup plotting traitors..."*

I called my wife from the military line and told her that I was at Akıncı Air Base and they should take care of themselves. I understood at the end of the incidents that my wife had shared this information with the authorities. When the TV was turned on two-to-three hours later, we learned that Parliament and police buildings had been bombarded. Besides, the planes were still in the air. I got angry and began to shout again. When they came back to the room, Ömer said they were ready to die if necessary. They all were like robots. When Mehmet Dişli came to me alone, I said the same thing to him. He said, they were not listening to him either. Admiral Ömer Harmancık was the one mainly speaking. As we watched statements by our president, prime minister and some ministers; people began to resist the coup at the risk of their lives; some soldiers had surrendered or were taken under control by the people or the police; the attitudes of four people in the room started to change. I spotted the hopelessness in their eyes. They were demoralized. I shouted out saying "You are in enough trouble. Just be a man and stop this madness. Stop other people dying. Before sunrise, withdraw your tanks and other military equipment from the streets. You disgraced us enough, do not go any further. What you did to us was worse than what the Balkan War did. You dishonored the armed forces. You will surrender to either the military prosecutor, public prosecutor or military police. Go and surrender and let me go". They did not answer. After a while there were some explosion noises outside. They themselves said that the landing fields were being bombarded. I observed that with time the traitors were getting more demoralized. I guess their hope disappeared as the tanks on Bosporus Bridge had surrendered and our president made a live address to a huge crowd at the Atatürk Airport.

*"There will be no negotiations..."*

I was shouting at their faces that there was nothing left

they could do, they cannot harm Turkish history and the Turkish Armed Forces any more than this, they were unsuccessful and now they needed to be mindful of young and innocent people, they needed to stop the air bombardment, they needed to send land troops to their barracks. I remember Kubilay and Mehmet were standing across me. They cringed. They were still not making any comments. Hence, they had fear and anxiety in their eyes. I guess it was 8:00 a.m. or 9:00 a.m. I told them again that it is possible to finish this without harming more people by surrendering and ending the coup and withdrawing all military units to their barracks. I also told them to put me in touch with either the prime minister or the president. In the meantime, the base was being bombarded from outside. They said "we will put you in touch". It may turn out to be an inextricable situation. They brought a cellphone and put me in touch with the prime minister. I told him about the situation. While speaking on the phone, looking them in the eye, I said, 'There will be no negotiations. They will surrender to either the military prosecutor, public prosecutor, police or military police'. I also called the NSC undersecretary and informed him about the situation."[17]

Akar's statements contain gruesome details. However, all these details are not enough to erase the questions in our minds about the coup night. Details such as Chief of General Staff Strategic Transformation Commander Major General Mehmet Dişli and Air Forces former Commander Akın Öztürk's connection to the coup plotters, and the visit by Sakarya Faculty of Theology teaching member Associate Professor Adil Öksüz, who was set free after a twenty-minute

---

[17] From July 15 record of statements.

interrogation despite being caught in the act at Akıncı Air Base, to Pennsylvania two days before the coup attempt await answers. By the way, Akıncı Air Base Commander General Hakan Evrim who wanted to put Chief of Staff Hulusi *Akar "in connection with Fetullah Gülen",* denied allegations and said *"I do not know Fetullah Gülen".* However the security surveillance camera footage from November 3, 2016 proved that General Hakan Evrim works in coordination with Adil Öksüz and Kemal Batmaz at Akıncı Air Base.[18]

---

[18] *Hürriyet* newspaper, Novermber 3, 2016.

# CONCLUSION

# HASAN SABBAH OF THE MODERN TIMES

Fetullah Gülen, who started up his community and community activities in 1965, has been a continuous actor in the last 50 years of Turkish political life. It would not be wrong to say that Fetullah Gülen built his life on paradoxes. He always had very good connections with politicians and the military, and had deep and secret arrangements with domestic and foreign intelligence services for pragmatic reasons. He was usually on the side of power and the powerful. He believes ends justify the means and hence, exploits religion and pious people. He sometimes appears as a 'hodja", sometimes as the leader of an organization with a hidden agenda. However we need to admit that all these paradoxes have some consistencies in their own context.

Basically, we have two different Gülen portraits. On the one hand, for the West, he is a wise man living the last days of his life; on the other hand, for his enemies, he is a Trojan Horse who wants to bring the Sharia rule to the world; a sick Turkish preacher. In Turkey, opinions about him differ slightly. For his followers he is an opinion leader who devoted his life to education and spreading Islam's universal language. For conservative people representing different Islamic factions, he is someone who distorts the main tenets of religion, legitimizes every means for his political aims, heretic in belief and attitude. He is also a false messiah, a Baha'i leader using Islam as an instrument. For Kemalists and secular circles, he is the leader of a radical Islamist group that is attempting to destroy the secular Republic for the sake of a religious one... Even the culmination of all these opposite characteristics in one person creates the perception that Gülen's "philosophy of life" is a created fiction or a project. Gülen, who build his whole life on "lies" and "deceptions," must have forgotten the saying, "System that are built on lies and exaggeration, even if they may last long, sooner or later collapse on to their founder's head."[1]

As a result, it is clear that Fetullah Gülen is not a man of religion and his organization is not a religious community. It has been precisely understood that the people who were suspicious about Gülen were proved right. After July 15, we witnessed that Gülen and his followers could be transformed into a dangerous and sickly terror organization that could kill innocent people without hesitation as long as they believe the circumstances are right to pursue their "cause". We had already seen in the December 17/25 process, just how cruel these "Bureaucratic Oligarchs", who received their orders from Gülen, could be. Audio recordings that were montaged, candid camera visuals from hotel rooms that violate privacy, people who lost their prestige by accusations based on fake documents, ammunition buried under the ground, assassinations and murders are all concrete evidences that demonstrate how this organization could turn into a wild crime machine. The unseen part of the iceberg surfaced after the night of July 15. It is against the nature of things to expect

---

[1]   Gülen, *Ölçü veya Yoldaki Işıklar*, p. 234.

Gülen to remain "clean" as he uses the same methods with underground illegal organizations and he has close ties with interesting figures such as Graham Fuller, Kasım Gülek, and Yaşar Tunagür. His relations with the military in the interim periods, his approach to different religions and communities as a part of interfaith dialogue, educational activities in Turkic Republics as a part of moderate Islam, and his close connections with the CIA, all show that Gülen has been used by international powers.

Seculars who state that religiosity is a danger after Gülen's real face has been revealed need to be asked one question: Do the architects of the periods in which people were not allowed to practice their religion freely, when religiosity was suppressed, have no role in Gülen's success of illegal activities? The Fetullah Gülen incident obliges Islamic circles as well as secular circles to comprehensive self-criticism. Since laicity that is essentially respectful towards religion and religious people is principal, then will those who are responsible for the years long wrong political practices be easily able to get out this resulting strangeness?

As of today, Gülen lost most of his pious and sincere supporters that he had been attracting for the last 50 years through the exploitation of religion. His close team that are part of his illegal activities had left Turkey before the coup attempt. Their activities abroad are continuing uninterruptedly. The United States administration prefers to act reluctantly on the Gülen issue. It is not easy to guess how the new president of the United States of America, Donald J. Trump, will act on this matter. If we think that Trump will be "tamed[2]" by the American deep state in the coming days, then we can

---

[2]  http://www.yenisafak.com/hayat/trumpi-islah-edecekler-2563330

assume that the future of Turkish-American relations will determine Gülen's future.

It is not just the US that acts reluctantly on Gülen; Europe, the Balkans, and some African countries compete to secretly give support to Gülen. When the strong position of the CIA is taken into consideration in these countries, to understand their political stance on the matter becomes easier. It is certain that the places to which Gülen's activities had reached will take their shares from this danger in the future. History will witness these countries confront the bitter truth sooner or later. The day will come, on which Fetullah Gülen, the modern day Hassan Sabbah,[3] will be brought to justice.

After the July 15 putsch, it is understood one more time that Turkey needs to eliminate figures and organizations that impose their distorted version of religion to people; exploit and misuse religion and religious people for their selfish gains; and creates schizophrenic deliriums. It is certain that nothing will remain the same after July 15 in Turkey. We are in a new period in which public recoinciliation and healing began. It is a process in which the common denominator will be the nation and moral values, the differences will be absorbed, and what is national and local will become important once again. However, there is one more point. It seems that the direct and indirect pressures and threat from the West and United States will increasingly continue. The biased attitude of Western media in recent times, Western politicians'

---

[3] A middle age leader in 11th century known for his cult, "Haşhaşiler" (the Assasins). Basing himself on a different religious tradition, Hassan Sabbah was an erudite man in religion, and authoritarian leader in his community. The cult he had established used military tactics based on assasination. He never left Alamut Castle for 34 years. Hasan Sabbah and his followers were succesful in transforming desires, disorderly beliefs and unbridled anger into an ideology and unprecedented harmony, discipline and intentional violence. For more see Bernard Lewis, *Haşhaşiler: İslam'da Radikal Bir Tarikat*, translation by Kemal Sarısözen, Kapı Publishing, Istanbul 2014.

attempts to provide sanctuaries for terrorists, and the rise of anti-Turkey feelings would give us some clues as to what awaits us in the future. For those seeking the opportunity to weaken Turkey, it would be not difficult to create new "Fetullah Gülens." Therefore, the goal of the New Turkey, which is united under the banner of patriotism, should be unity and brotherhood, republic and democracy, soverignity and freedom, and free judicary and justice.

Gülen owes his fame to former CHP Secretary-General Kasım Gülek. His close relations with Gülek reveal, perhaps, the darkest episode in his life. (From left to right: Cem Karaca, Kasım Gülek and Fethullah Gülen)

*The Washington Times* writer Abraham Wagner followed Gülen closely. His statements on Gülen and his community are noteworthy.

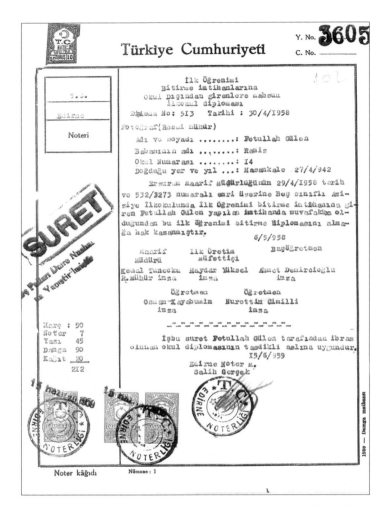

Though he gets the Green Card through the "talented educator" status in 2008, Gülen graduated from elementary school in 1958 at the age of 17. We need to accept the fact that a person who graduates from elementary school really does have "special talents".

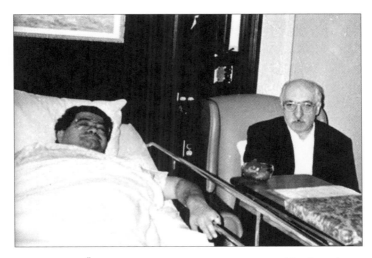

Gülen visits late Özal in the hospital after a serious heart operation. Gülen likes to have photos taken with right-wing politicians. His path intersected with Özal after the 1980 coup.

It is very rare to have a politician who would *"fail in respect for"* Gülen. It is again for the future of Turkey that President Erdoğan had the courage to fight Gülen against all odds.

Gülen, starts interreligious dialogue officially by meeting with Pope Jean Paul II on February 8, 1998. Former owner of *Zaman* Newspaper Alaattin Kaya and Jesuit Minister Thomas Michel were also present at the meeting. The person who organized the appointment at the Vatican still remains a mystery.

Gülen's daily, *Zaman*, published a headline targeting the Vatican seven years prior to Gülen's meeting with the Pope. The news on missionary activities is still in the archives of newspaper. May 23, 1991

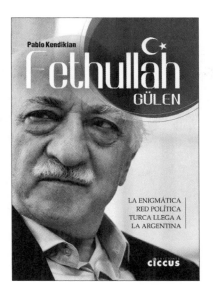

The latest book by Argentinian Armenian Pablo Kendikian that analyzes Gülen's secret political targets.

Fuller insistently rejects claims that Gülen and his community is a cult. He prefers to define the community as *"The Most encouraging face of modern-day Islam"*

Gülen's negative rhetoric on Prime Minister Erbakan and the Welfare Party, to protect himself and his community, were in the headlines of various newspapers. His attitude and rhetoric are not surprising as he always sides with the "powerful" ones.

After July 15, U.S. media made news that underestimate Turkish claims. They tried to create the perception that a person living abroad as an exile, cannot be behind the coup attempt.

Gülen's statements in the headlines of *Hürriyet* daily reflect not only his opinions but also the opinions of *Hürriyet*. Although they try to gloss over it now, the Turkish media failed at the democracy test on February 28.

# THE TIMES

### Best for sport

Tensions rise as three US police shot dead in 'heinous' ambush

May appeals
to Labour:
Don't gamble
with Trident

## Presidential power grab
## after failed Turkish coup

Erdogan cracks down on judiciary and military

# Mail Online

Home | News | U.S. | Sport | TV&Showbiz | Australia | Femail | Health | Science | Money | Video | Travel | Fashion Finder

'They will pay a heavy price for their treason': Turkish soldiers
surrender on Bosphorus Bridge after overnight military coup
FAILS, ending with 90 dead and President Erdogan vowing reve

## PAYBACK TIM

BREAKING NEWS

Turkey President Erdogan declares military coup attempt over, says government is in control.

# Erdogan: Coup over

Night of chaos

VIDEO: Explosions on the street

CNN Turk taken off air by soldiers

PM: Military taking illegal action

Turkey's long history of coups

Currency plunges on coup

Who is President Erdogan?

LATEST: At least 42 dead, images of military surrender
Turkey coup: Gunfire, explosions, confusion | 'Government in control' | Coup attempt shocking

On the coup night, the foreign media waited a long time to act against the coup. Although
the coup attempt was suppressed at midnight, the headlines could only be written at
dawn. CNN's attitude towards the coup plotters taken into custody was noteworthy:
*"Democracy is under pressure in Turkey"*.

Fox News ☉
@FoxNews

Lt. Col. Peters on #Turkey: "If the coup
succeeds, Islamists lose and we win."
#OReillyFactor

LT. COL. RALPH PETERS (RET.)
FOX NEWS STRATEGIC ANALYST

RETWEETS     LIKES
1,661         1,743

New York Times World ☉
@nytimesworld

"The Erdogan supporters are sheep, and they
will follow whatever he says." nyti.ms/2a7LOk8

The attitude of Western media after the coup creates disappointment for the future. On
one hand, *The New York Times* accuses Erdoğan supporters of acting like "sheep", on the
other hand, *Fox News* serves news like "Had the coup been successful, we would have
won". There is nothing much to say.

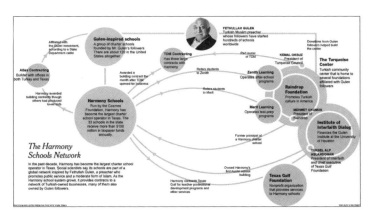

The table published in *The New York Times*, showing Gülen and his community's
educational activities in the US.

Adil Öksüz who was the key figure behind the coup, was caught at Akıncı Air Base. In court, he said that he was there to look for some property to buy, and he was thus released. It is understood now that he was not the imam of the air force but the imam of the main military headquarters. Nobody knows where Öksüz was on the night of the coup.

As many as 248 people died on the night of July 15, 2016. Most of the deceased were civilians. Crazed coup plotters swept over everything. However, the efforts of the public prevented the coup plotters from reaching their goal.

The victory celebration after the morning of June 15 turned Turkey in to a carnival area. Squares, where thousands of flags were waving in the sky, hosted the pro-democracy demonstrations for months. *Istanbul, Taksim Atatürk Monument.*

# BIBLIOGRAPHY

AKMAN, Nuriye, Interview with Fetullah Gülen on January 28, 1995 in *Sabah* newspaper.

AKİNAN, Serdar, Doç. Dr. Hakan Yavuz ile Bir Sohbet, *Sky Türk*, July 2008. http://arsiv.gercekgundem.com/?p=144531

AVCI, Hanefi, *Haliç'te Yaşayan Simonlar, Dün Devlet Bugün Cemaat*, Angora Publishing, Ankara 2010.

BAŞBUĞ, İlker, *15 Temmuz Öncesi ve Sonrası*, Doğan Book, Istanbul 2016.

BERNARD, Cheryl, *Civil Democratic Islam: Partners, Resources and Strategies*, RAND, US 2003. http://www.rand.org/content/dam/rand/pubs/monograph_reports/2005/MR1716.pdf

BERK, Bekir, *Çağ ve Nesil* journal, No. 9, May 1984.

BERLINSKI, Claire, "Who is Fetullah Gulen", *City Journal*, 2012.

BULUT, Faik, *Kim Bu Fetullah Gülen*, Berfin Publishing, Istanbul 2016.

CANİKLİGİL, Razi, *ABD Gizli Belgelerinde Fetullah Gülen*, Doğan Books, Istanbul 2016.

ÇAKIR, Ruşen, *Ayet ve Slogan*, Metis Publishing, Istanbul 1990.

..............., Semih Sakallı, *Yüz Soruda Erdoğan x Gülen Savaşı*, Metis Publishing, Istanbul 2014.

ÇETİNKAYA, Hikmet, *Fetullah Gülen'in 40 Yıllık Serüveni*, Cumhuriyet Books, Istanbul 2014.

ÇOBANOĞLU, Yavuz, "Asenası Eksik Bir Hareket: Gülen Cemaa-ti", *Birikim* dergisi, October 2012, No. 282.

..............., *Altın Neslin Peşinde*, İletişim Publsihing, Istanbul 2012.

..............., "Fetullah Gülen'in Eğitim ve Ahlâk Anlayışına Eleştirel Bir Bakış", *Eğitim, Bilim, Toplum* Dergisi, Spring, no. 6 (2008), 22.

ÇORAKLI, Selim, *Darbelerin Efendisi Hocia*, Eftalya Publishing, Istanbul 2016.

DUMAN, Doğan, *Demokrasi Sürecinde Türkiye'de İslamahk*, Dokuz Eylül Publishing, Istanbul 1999.

DUMANLI, Ekrem, *Zaman* newspaper March 7, 2011.

ERDOĞAN, Latif, *Fetullah Gülen, Küçük Dünyam*, Ufuk Publishing, Istanbul 2006.

EVREN, Kenan, Diyarbakır speech dated October 14, 1980.

..............., Konya speech dated January 15, 1981.

FULLER, Graham E., *Türkiye ve Arap Baharı*, trans. Mustafa Acar, Eksi Books, Ankara 2014.

..............., *The Future of Political Islam*, Palgrave Macmillan, US 2003.

Gazeteciler ve Yazarlar Vakfı, April 2013, Media announcement

GEZİCİ, Aytekin, *Okyanus Ötesi Gerçeği*, Anatolia Book, Istanbul 2011.

GÜLEN, Fetullah, *Asrın Getirdiği Tereddütler 3*, Nil Publishing, İzmir 1985.

..............., *Çağ ve Nesil 1*, Nil Publishing, İzmir 1982.

..............., *Fasıldan Fasıla 1*, Nil Publishing, İzmir 2006

..............., *Fasıldan Fasıla 3*, Nil Publishing, İzmir 2009.

..............., *İ'lâ-yı Kelimetullah veya Cihad*, Nil Publishing, İzmir 2001.

..............., *İnanan Gölgesinde 2*, Nil Publishing, İzmir 1993.

..............., *Ölçü veya Yoldaki Işıklar*, Nil Publishing, İzmir 2011.

..............., *Prizma 1*, Nil Yayınları, 3rd edition, İzmir 1996.

..............., *Prizma 2*, Nil Publishing, İzmir 2010.

..............., *Ümit Burcu (Kırk Testi 4)*, Nil Publishing, İzmir 2005.

..............., Friday Preach at İzmir Hisar Mosque (November 26, 1989).

HABLEMİTOĞLU, Necip, *Köstebek*, Pozitif Publishing, Istanbul 2016.

LEWIS, Bernard, *Haşhaşiler: İslam'da Radikal Bir Tarikat*, çev. Kemal Sarısözen, Kapı Publishing, Istanbul 2014.

MEVLÂNÂ, *Mesnevî-i Şerîf*, müt. Süleyman Nahîfî, sad. Âmil Çelebioğlu, Timaş Publishing, Istanbul 2007.

ÖZÇELİK, Can, *Kâinat İmam Fetullah Gülen*, Destek Publishing, Istanbul 2014.

ÖZKÖK, Ertuğrul, Interview with Fetullah Gülen between January 23-28, 1995 in *Hürriyet* newspaper.

ÖZSOY, Osman, Mim Kemal Öke, *Samanyolu TV*, 29.03.1997.

POYRAZ, Ergün, *İhanet ve Darbe*, Bilgi Publishing House, Istanbul 2016.

..............., *İndeki Vaiz*, Tanyeri Books, Istanbul 2014.

RUBIN, Michael, "Erdoğan prepares for a bloodbath", https://www.aei.org/publication/erdogan-prepares-for-a-bloodbath/

RUMSFELD, Donald, *Known and Unknown a Memoir*, Penguin Group, 2012.

SENEM, Nusret, *Fetullah Gülen'in Konuşmaları ve Pensilvanya İfadesi*, Kaynak Publishing, Istanbul 2012.

SEVİNDİ, Nevval, *Fetullah Gülen ile New York Sohbeti*, Sabah Books, Istanbul 1997.

ŞENER, Nedim, *Ergenekon Belgelerinde Fetullah Gülen ve Cemaat*, Destek Publishing, Istanbul 2016.

ŞIK, Ahmet, *Paralel Yürüdük Biz Bu Yollarda*, Postacı Publishing House, Istanbul 2014.

THOMAS MICHEL, S.J., "Sufism and Modernity in the Thought of Fetullah Gülen", *The Muslim World*, Special Edition, July2005, Vol. 95, No: 3, pp 341-358.

*The New York Times*, 25 July 2016, Fetullah Gulen: I Condemn All Threats to Turkey's Democracy.

TOKALAK, İsmail, *Korku İmparatorluğu*, Asi Publishing, Istanbul 2016.

TURGUT, Hulusi, *Yeni Yüzyıl*, article dated January 15-February 3, 1998.

YAVUZ, M. Hakan, "Devlete İnanırım, Devletçi Değilim", Fetullah Gülen interview, *Milliyet*, August 11, 1997.

YEŞİLYURT, Süleyman, *Pensilvanya Canbazı*, Alter Publishing, Istanbul 2014.

**Court Documents**

Records of 2nd State Security Court of Ankara, Indicment, August 31, 2001, Dossier no: 2000/124 E

Records of 2nd State Security Court of Ankara, Defense, August 31, 2001, Dossier no: 2000/124 E.

Ankara Office of Chief Public Prosecutor, Fetullah Gülen criminal charges Dossier no :2000/420

Private Archieves, Deciphered from audio cassette 1, Nuh Mete Yüksel.

**Periodicals**

*Hürriyet* newspaper, 03.11.2016.

*Star* newspaper, 10 Şubat 2014.

*Takvim* newspaper, 10 Mart 2014,

*Taraf* newspaper, 14 Ocak 2008.

*Yeni Şafak* newspaper

**Online References**

http://fehmikoru.com/cemaat-icinde-derin-cemaat-var-derdim-bu-gun-artik-diyemiyorum-sebebi-su/

http://fgulen.com/tr/turk-basininda-Fetullah-gulen/Fetullah-gu-lenle-tv-dergi-roportajlari/Fetullah-gulen-televizyon-roporta-jlari/1463-Kanal-D-Kanal-Dde-Yalcin-Dogana-Verdigi-Mu-lakat

http://fgulen.org/about-Fetullah-gulen/gulens-thoughts/1294-the-new-man-and-woman.html

http://freedomoutpost.com/worlds-most-dangerous-islamist-alive-well-and-living-in-pennsylvania/

http://herkul.org/herkul-nagme/402-nagme-birlik-dirlik-ve-beraberligin-yolu/

http://odatv.com/fbidan-Fetullah-gulen-sorusturma-si--2709131200.html

http://odatv.com/kadinlar-cehennemin-etrafini-ceviren-seyle-rdir--0906121200.html

http://rusencakir.com/Fetullah-Gulen-Butun-Alevilerin-ayaklari-nin-altina-basimi-rahatlikla-koyabilirim/2065

http://thehill.com/blogs/congress-blog/homeland-security/264031-turkey-justified-in-seeking-extradition-of-us-based

http://tr.fgulen.com/content/view/2257/141/

http://tr.fgulen.com/content/view/3178/132

http://tr.fgulen.com/content/view/3500/128/

http://tr.fgulen.com/content/view/7877/15/

http://www.bbc.com/turkce/haberler/2014/06/140620_graham_fuller_roportaj

http://www.boilingfrogspost.com/2016/07/18/newsbud-sibel-ed-monds-dissects-the-turkey-coup-attempt-a-cia-gulen-concoct-ed-dry-run/

http://www.cnnturk.com/2012/turkiye/10/07/diyanet.isleri.bas-kanindan.alevilik.aciklamasi/679605.0/index.html

http://www.diarioarmenia.org.ar/el-movimiento-gulen-al-descu-bierto-trama-y-objetivos/

http://www.haber7.com/haber.php?haber_id=121422

http://www.huffingtonpost.com/graham-e-fuller/gulen-move-ment-not-cult_b_11116858.html

http://www.medyagundem.com/fetonun-abddeki-tetikcisi-nin-son-skandali/

http://www.milliyet.com.tr/balkanlar-daki-feto-dunya-2285462/

http://www.mynet.com/haber/guncel/gulen-basortusune-tefer-ruat-dedi-mi-898284-1

http://www.nationalreview.com/article/224182/turkeys-turning-point-michael-rubin

http://www.ntv.com.tr/dunya/Fetullah-gulen-israilden-izin-almaliydilar,kIC_HTknIEavwlzh-VOxdg

http://www.ntv.com.tr/turkiye/cumhurbaskanligi-sozcusu-kalin-karanlik-baslayan-gece-aydinlik-olarak-tarihimize,6qugeweFJkidrfrUxhexVg

http://www.sizinti.com.tr/konular/ayrinti/son-karakol.html

http://www.sizinti.com.tr/konular/ayrinti/yollari-gozlenen-bir-nesil-bir-kitap-nasil-okunmali.html

http://www.sizinti.com.tr/konular/ayrınti/asker.html

http://www.spiegel.de/international/germany/guelen-movement-accused-of-being-a-sect-a-848763.html

http://www.star.com.tr/acikgorus/turkiyenin-burokratik-oligark-ile-imtihani-haber-1121023/

http://www.takvim.com.tr/guncel/2014/03/10/cia-demek-cemaat-demek

http://www.theatlantic.com/international/archive/2013/08/a-rare-meeting-with-reclusive-turkish-spiritual-leader-Fetullah-gulen/278662/

http://www.timeturk.com/tr/2014/02/27/cia-erdogani-neden-hedef-aldi.html

http://www.voanews.com/a/Fetullah-gulen-/3421616.html

http://www.washingtontimes.com/news/2016/jan/21/abraham-wagner-gulen-movement-a-threat-to-us-turke/

http://www.yenisafak.com/arsiv/2000/ekim/16/dizi.html

http://www.yenisafak.com/hayat/trumpi-islah-edecekler-2563330

https://counterjihadreport.com/2013/08/30/more-dangerous-than-bin-laden-protestors-to-descend-on-gulens-mountain-fortress-in-pennsylvania/

https://newrepublic.com/article/79062/global-turkey-imam-Fetullah-gulen

https://www.aei.org/publication/could-there-be-a-coup-in-turkey/

https://www.aei.org/publication/erdogan-prepares-for-a-bloodbath/

https://www.aei.org/publication/the-next-phase-in-turkeys-political-violence/

https://www.commentarymagazine.com/foreign-policy/middle-east/reconsidering-Fetullah-gulen/

https://www.commonwealmagazine.org/why-turkey-targeting-hizmet

https://www.youtube.com/watch?v=gRx8S5YTdJk&feature=youtu.be&app=desktop

https://www.youtube.com/watch?v=lqLt6XxByJs

https://www.youtube.com/watch?v=yf0P_80Jlxk

www.bbc.co.uk/turkce/haberler/2014/01/140126_Fetullah_gulen_roportaj_guney.shtml

www.f-gulen.org.

www.herkul.org/herkul-nagme/391-nagme-egitime-darbe-plani

# INDEX